GOOD HOUSEKEEPING
easy 30-MINUTE
DINNERS

GOOD HOUSEKEEPING
easy 30-MINUTE
DINNERS

85 DELISH RECIPES FOR BUSY COOKS & STRESS-FREE WEEKNIGHTS

© 2020 by Hearst Magazines, Inc.

Book design by Joanna Williams

Library of Congress Cataloging-in-Publication Data is on file with the publisher.

978-92-1-950099-74-0

2 4 6 8 10 9 7 5 3 1 paperback

HEARST

CONTENTS

RECIPES

③ SIMPLE SHEET PAN DINNERS 93

RECIPES

4 NO-SWEAT GRILLING 133

RECIPES

5 BONUS: AWESOME AIR FRYER 175

RECIPES

Mediterranean Chicken Bake, recipe on p 99

A LETTER FROM
THE EDITORS OF GOOD HOUSEKEEPING

With so many kitchen tools to choose from these days, it can be a serious struggle to know which to use and how to use it to make mealtime easy any day of the week. We're taking the guesswork out of dinnertime and giving you tips and tricks to use our favorite tools plus plenty of recipes guaranteed to help you get dinner on the table in record time.

In this book, you'll find the best no-fuss meals for your family using four of the most versatile kitchen tools you probably already have at home—a skillet, a multi-cooker, a sheet pan, and a grill. We're also throwing in bonus air fryer recipes for fun, better-for-you dinners the whole family will love, as well as sides to take your quick-and-easy dinner to the next level, and a few desserts so you cap your night off with a sweet treat.

Let's get cooking!

XOXO,

The GH Food Editors

Dijon Pork & Asparagus Sauté, recipe on p 31

1

SKILLET SUPPERS

When you're pressed for time, the humble skillet might just be your go-to kitchen tool. This mighty pan browns meat so beautifully while building robust flavor so you can put the best beef, pork and lamb dinners on the table in no time! The best part of it all is that using one pan means less cleanup—and for the busy cook, that is reason enough to grab a skillet and get cooking.

SIX SKILLET MUST-HAVES

Our skillet dishes are super easy, but it still takes the right pan to do the job. Use this quick checklist to make sure you're using the best skillet for flawless results every time.

- **SIZE.** Our pick is a 12-inch skillet. For food to properly brown (versus steam), the skillet must be roomy enough to hold what's cooking in a single layer with at least one inch between the pieces.
- **ROLLED RIM.** This helps transfer saucy dishes to serving plates without dripping.
- **BALANCE.** A 12-inch skillet is large, so a well-designed handle will make it feel balanced. A helper-handle (a small loop handle opposite the main handle) makes lifting a lot easier, too.

⬤ **STAY-COOL HANDLE.** To get a comfortable grip, heat shouldn't travel more than a couple inches up the handle.

⬤ **HEATS EVENLY.** Heat should spread from the area directly over the flame to the pan's outer edges without overheating in the center.

⬤ **KEEPS HEAT STEADY.** A heavy-bottomed skillet does a better job maintaining steady surface temperature at high or low heats, which allows more control when cooking.

NONSTICK SKILLETS

If your tolerance for cleaning is really low—read: nonexistent—it's best to go nonstick. They're manufactured with a chemical-compound coating that's applied to aluminum or stainless steel that makes food slip easily off its surface. Chances are, you already own one (nonstick cookware makes up about 70 percent of the cookware market). However, there are a few caveats to cooking in a nonstick skillet. Here's the lowdown:

PROS

- Foods don't stick, which is great for egg dishes and for delicate fish dishes.
- Cleanup is easy with no bits or stains to scrub.

GOOD TO KNOW

- It's best to use over medium heat (medium-high max). On high heat, the finish can give off unhealthy fumes (but experts say that as long as the pan's temperature is below 500°F, it's harmless).
- Broiling or searing can be problematic with the no-high-heat rule. You can use a nonstick skillet with a ceramic coating which is the safer option over high heat, but the surface isn't as stick-proof.
- Don't heat a nonstick skillet when it's empty.
- Don't use nonstick cooking sprays. You'll end up with gunky buildup that will detract from rather than enhance the finish.
- Replace pans that begin to flake. Our pick? A heavy-bottomed skillet with more

than one layer of nonstick coating—it does a better job of retaining heat and browning food.

PAN HANDLING

- To avoid chipping or damaging the pan, use wooden spoons and silicone or nylon tipped tongs to stir and pick up food, avoid steel wool, and don't stack them right on top of each other. If you need to, put a paper towel liner between them.
- To ensure the nonstick coating lasts on your skillet, gentle cleaning to avoid scratching the surface is essential. Wash in hot, soapy water using a sponge or nylon scrub pad.
- Teflon-free skillets with ceramic, hard anodized aluminum, or hybrid material coating clean up beautifully whether you hand-wash or use the dishwasher.

STAINLESS STEEL SKILLETS

Stainless steel skillets are produced using a three-ply bond core that incorporates an aluminum center. That makes the pan a great conductor of heat.

PROS

- Searing is fine. Brown steaks over high heat without worrying about fumes.
- Durability is superior due to its construction.
- Sleek styles from high-end brands boast a hand-polished, mirror-finish exterior.

GOOD TO KNOW

- Food can stick if the pan is not heated correctly.

PAN HANDLING

- Cool the skillet slightly then immerse in warm water.
- Apply a paste of nonabrasive powder cleanser mixed with water and rub in a circular motion from the center outward with a sponge or nylon scrub pad.
- Wash the pan in hot, soapy water, rinse well, and dry thoroughly.

CAST-IRON SKILLETS

It's the type of kitchenware that tends to get passed down through generations. But if you didn't inherit Granny's cast-iron pan, here's why it's time to buy one and start your own family tradition.

PROS

- It gets better with age, even after years of heavy use. As you cook in a cast-iron skillet, the pan gradually takes on a natural slick patina that releases food easily.
- It's virtually indestructible and can easily be restored if mistreated.
- Heat retention is a special talent, making cast-iron ideal for browning, searing and shallow frying.
- New cookware is preseasoned. This coating keeps the skillet from rusting or reacting with acidic food and helps food release more easily.

GOOD TO KNOW

- It's slow to heat up and can have hot spots.
- It's heavy, which is a bit of a challenge when transferring the pan from stove to oven or from cooking to serving. Use a towel or potholder when taking a skillet out of the oven or moving it on the stovetop.
- It needs maintenance. Without proper care, cast-iron cookware can rust.

SKILLET S.O.S.

Bought a rusty pan from a yard sale? Does your pan look dry and patchy? It's not too late to bring your cast-iron surface back to life. Here's how:

- ❯ **RINSE** skillet in hot water (no soap); remove rust with a plastic brush, then dry with paper towels.
- ❯ **COAT** skillet, inside and out, with vegetable oil or shortening.
- ❯ **PLACE** skillet upside down on a cookie sheet and bake at 350°F for 1 hour.
- ❯ **COOL** skillet completely on a wire rack. Wipe all surfaces with paper towels.

PAN HANDLING

- Rinse with hot water and a scrub brush (avoid abrasive powder, harsh soap and don't leave the pan soaking). You can also mix kosher salt with oil to make a DIY scrubber that can remove stuck-on food.

- Wipe the clean pan all over with paper towels and place over medium-low heat until all the moisture disappears.

- Add a few drops of vegetable oil and rub the inside of the skillet with paper towels until it's shiny but not sticky.

SKILLET SKILLS

THE PAN SEAR

Pan searing is cooking meat (poultry and fish) in a skillet over moderately high to high heat for a short period of time. And because pan-seared meat is turned only once, the meat has time to develop a flavorful crust while keeping it moist and juicy inside. To pan sear like a pro, follow these rules:

- Pat meat dry with paper towels before seasoning. Excess moisture interferes with searing.

- Heat oil in a large, heavy-bottomed skillet (big enough to hold the food in a single layer with at least 1 inch between the pieces) for at least 2 min. or until hot. The oil should ripple slightly before you add the meat. (Note: If there is no oil in the recipe, a drop of water should sizzle on contact with the pan.)

- Add meat to the hot skillet. Don't move the meat for at least 2 to 3 min. or until it turns brown from the bottom up. This will release the juices to the surface of the meat, where they will caramelize, giving good color and flavor to the dish.

- Turn meat over. Continue cooking to desired doneness.

- Transfer meat to serving plates as soon as it is done to prevent overcooking. For larger steaks that will be sliced before serving, let meat stand on a cutting board for 5 min. to allow the juices to redistribute in the meat.

THE WAY TO SAUTÉ

Sauter, the French verb for "jump," is literally what happens when food cooks quickly in a skillet. Sautéing browns meat (poultry or fish) on the outside until cooked through. Depending on the size of the ingredients, the food is either stirred often or occasionally, unlike pan searing, where you only turn the meat once. Use the following technique for perfectly sautéed chicken.

- Heat oil (or melt butter) in large skillet (big enough to hold the food in a single layer with at least 1 inch between the pieces) over medium (for nonstick) or medium-high heat for at least 1 minute or until hot.
- Add seasoned or coated chicken to hot skillet. Wait for 1 to 2 min. or until chicken turns brown before stirring.
- Turn or stir chicken several times until cooked through.
- Remove chicken from the skillet with slotted spoon.

THE SECRET TO GREAT SAUCE

Don't clean the pan right away! Sautéed chicken leaves behind flavorful browned bits (called *fond*), which is the foundation of a pan sauce. Add broth, wine or tomatoes to the pan; bring to boiling. Reduce heat and simmer, stirring with a wooden spoon, until browned bits are loosened from bottom of pan. Voila! You're done.

VEGGIE SKILLET SKILLS

Just like meat, poultry and fish, skillet veggies have their own set of rules.

- **CHOOSE TENDER VEGGIES.** Sautéed veggies don't spend much time in the skillet. Softer vegetables like mushrooms, bell peppers, baby artichokes and sugar snap peas can go directly in the skillet. For denser vegetables like beets, boil them briefly in salted water before sautéing to get a head start on the cooking.
- **CUT VEGGIES INTO BITE-SIZE PIECES.** Vegetables that are too large will more likely burn or form a tough, overly browned crust by the time they're properly cooked.
- **STIR AT THE RIGHT TIME.** Mix tender veggies frequently to promote even browning and cooking. Denser vegetables like cubed potatoes should be stirred once every few minutes so that they don't fall apart as they grow tender.

SKILLET RECIPES

FIERY KUNG PAO CHICKEN

Forget takeout — this homemade Chinese-inspired recipe, made with chicken and spicy chiles in your favorite cast-iron skillet, packs all pao. Kung pao, that is.

¼	cup unsweetened rice wine
¼	cup low-sodium soy sauce
1	Tbsp cornstarch
1½	lbs boneless, skinless chicken thighs, trimmed and cut into 1-in. pieces
1	Tbsp canola oil
1	bunch scallions, thinly sliced
3	cloves garlic, finely chopped
1	2-in. piece fresh ginger, finely chopped
3	Tbsp balsamic vinegar
8	whole dried chiles de árbol
½	cup roasted unsalted peanuts
	Cooked rice and cilantro, for serving

Active time: 15 min.

Total time: 30 min.

Serves: 4

About 260 calories
13 g fat (2 g sat)
27 g pro
700 mg sodium
9 g carb
2 g fiber

1. In medium bowl, whisk together rice wine, soy sauce and cornstarch until smooth. Add chicken and toss to coat; let stand 30 min. or refrigerate up to 1 hr.

2. Heat oil in large skillet on medium-high. Add scallions, garlic and ginger and cook, tossing until garlic is golden brown, 2 to 3 min.

3. Add chicken (and marinade) and cook, stirring often until chicken is cooked through, 3 to 5 min.

4. Stir in vinegar, chiles and peanuts and cook, stirring for 2 min. Serve with rice and top with cilantro, if desired.

MEDITERRANEAN BAKED COD

This saucy cod dish gets a touch of sweetness from jammy peppers and onions.

1	medium onion, thinly sliced
6	oz mini sweet peppers
	Kosher salt and pepper
1	Tbsp extra-virgin olive oil
1	pint grape tomatoes, halved
8	sprigs fresh thyme
4	6-oz pieces cod fillet

Active time: 10 min.

Total time: 20 min.

Serves: 4

About 205 cal
5 g fat (1 g sat)
32 g pro
115 mg sodium
8 g carb
1 g fiber

1. Heat oven to 450°F. Heat oil in large oven-safe skillet on medium-high. Add onion, peppers, and ¼ tsp each salt and pepper and cook, stirring occasionally until onion is nearly tender, 5 to 6 min.

2. Add tomatoes and thyme and cook 2 min.; stir in ¼ cup water. Season cod with ¼ tsp salt and nestle among vegetables. Cover skillet, transfer to oven and roast until cod is opaque throughout, 12 to 15 min.

FISH FACTS: IS IT DONE?

Cooking fish in a skillet requires quick thinking. No problem! Just follow this guide for perfect results.

> **THIN FISH FILLETS (RED SNAPPER, TILAPIA, SEA BASS OR CATFISH):** When the outside is opaque, the fish is done.
> **THICK FISH FILLETS (SALMON, COD OR HALIBUT):** Gently insert a small thin knife into the thickest part of the fillet to see if it's just opaque throughout.
> **SHRIMP:** Color turns from translucent grey to just opaque and pearly pink.
> **SEA SCALLOPS:** Cut into one scallop with the tip of a knife; it should be just opaque.

CHICKEN WITH CREAMY SPINACH & ARTICHOKES

Browned artichoke hearts and garlicky greens dress
up this quick weeknight staple.

2	Tbsp olive oil, divided
4	6-oz boneless, skinless chicken breasts
	Kosher salt and pepper
1	lemon, halved
1	14-oz can artichoke hearts, drained, patted dry and halved
2	cloves garlic, thinly sliced
1/2	cup dry white wine
1/4	cup sour cream
1	bunch spinach, thick stems discarded

Active time: 20 min.

Total time: 30 min.

Serves: 4

About 305 cal
11.5 g fat (3 g sat)
38 g pro
675 mg sodium
10 g carb
2 g fiber

1. Heat 1 Tbsp oil in large skillet on medium. Season chicken with 1/2 tsp each salt and pepper and cook until golden brown and cooked through, 6 to 8 min. per side. Transfer to plates and squeeze lemon juice on top.

2. Add remaining Tbsp oil to skillet and heat on medium-high. Add artichokes, cut-side down, and cook 3 min.

3. Lower heat to medium; toss with garlic. Stir in wine and cook 2 min. Stir in sour cream and spinach leaves, season with pinch each salt and pepper and cook until just wilted.

SHRIMP BOIL WITH SAUSAGE & SPINACH

Microwaving the potatoes first makes this a fast feast to get
on the table—and onto your fork.

1	lb small red-skinned new potatoes (about 12)
2	Tbsp olive oil
1	large onion, chopped
	Kosher salt and pepper
4	oz kielbasa, sliced
2	cloves garlic, finely chopped
1	tsp ground coriander
1/2	tsp ground mustard
1/4	tsp cayenne
3/4	lb large peeled and deveined shrimp (about 16)
1	cup corn kernels (from 1 ear, or thawed if frozen)
1	bunch spinach (about 12 oz), thick stems discarded, leaves roughly chopped

Active time: 15 min.

Total time: 20 min.

Serves: 4

About 345 calories
13 g fat (3 g sat)
21 g pro
1,125 mg sodium
35 g carb
4 g fiber

1. Place potatoes on plate and microwave on High, 2 min. Turn
and microwave until just tender, 1 to 2 min. more. Cut in half.

2. Meanwhile, heat oil in large nonstick skillet on medium. Add
onion and 1/2 tsp each salt and pepper and cook, stirring
occasionally, until onion is tender, 4 to 6 min. Add potatoes and
cook, stirring occasionally, until light golden brown, 2 to 3 min.
Push to one side of pan.

3. Add kielbasa to other side of pan and cook, stirring
occasionally, until starting to brown, 3 to 4 min. Add garlic,
coriander, mustard and cayenne and cook, tossing, 1 min.

4. Add shrimp, corn and spinach; cover and cook, shaking pan
occasionally, until shrimp are opaque throughout, 2 to 3 min.

HOW TO PEEL & DEVEIN SHRIMP

Mastering this technique is easier than you think.

1. Starting at the head end of the shrimp, peel off all the shell and, if desired, the tail.

2. With a small knife, make a cut along the center of the back of the shrimp to expose the vein.

3. Use the knife to pull out the vein.

THAI BEEF & VEGGIE STIR-FRY

Thinly slicing the beef ensures quick-cooking bites,
while curry paste brings bold flavor.

1	lb beef sirloin
	Kosher salt
1	Tbsp olive oil
1/4	cup Thai green curry paste
1	13.5-oz can unsweetened light coconut milk
8	oz green beans, trimmed and halved
1	8-oz can bamboo shoots, rinsed
	Cooked rice and basil, for serving

Active time: 20 min.

Total time: 25 min.

Serves: 4

About 390 cal
27 g fat (11.5 g sat)
25 g pro
800 mg sodium
13 g carb
2 g fiber

1. Thinly slice beef and season with 1/4 tsp salt.

2. Heat oil in large skillet on medium-high and swirl; then add beef and cook until browned, 2 to 3 min. per side, and transfer to a plate.

3. Add curry paste and cook, stirring, for 2 min. Whisk in coconut milk and bring to a simmer.

4. Add green beans and cook until just tender, 3 to 4 min.

5. Return beef to skillet along with bamboo shoots and cook until heated through. Serve over rice and sprinkle with basil, if desired.

KITCHEN TIP *Heat ready-to-serve jasmine rice according to package directions, top with the curry then garnish with thinly sliced fresh basil leaves.*

OIL & VINEGAR CHICKEN CUTLET SANDWICHES

Hearty baguette holds up well to the juicy chicken and vinegar-soaked onions. You can also pack this sandwich in the morning and it'll be good for lunch!

½	small red onion, thinly sliced
1	Tbsp red wine vinegar
	Kosher salt and pepper
1	lb boneless, skinless chicken breasts
1	Tbsp olive oil
6	cups baby spinach
1	large baguette, cut in 4 5-in. pieces and each split and toasted

Active time: 20 min.

Total time: 20 min.

Serves: 4

About 330 cal
7 g fat (1 g sat)
33 g pro
705 mg sodium
32 g carb
3 g fiber

1. In small bowl, toss onion with vinegar and ⅛ tsp each salt and pepper; let sit, tossing occasionally, until ready to use.

2. Cut chicken into 6 thin cutlets. Season chicken with ½ tsp each salt and pepper and cook until browned and cooked through, 2 min. per side; transfer to cutting board.

3. Add spinach to skillet, season with salt and pepper and cook until just beginning to wilt, 2 to 3 min.

4. Slice chicken and sandwich between baguette halves with spinach and onions.

DIJON PORK & ASPARAGUS SAUTÉ

Tarragon-seasoned pork in a white wine-mustard sauce makes
an easy yet elegant weeknight option.

2	**Tbsp fresh tarragon leaves, chopped**
	Kosher salt and pepper
4	**6-oz boneless pork chops**
2	**Tbsp olive oil**
1	**lb asparagus, sliced on an angle**
1	**bunch scallions, sliced**
½	**cup dry white wine**
1	**Tbsp Dijon mustard**

Active time: 10 min.

Total time: 15 min.

Serves: 4

About 455 cal
31 g fat (9 g sat)
37 g pro
470 mg sodium
7 g carb
2 g fiber

1. In small bowl, combine tarragon and ½ tsp salt. Rub all over pork chops.

2. Heat oil in large skillet on medium-high. Add pork and cook until browned, 2 to 3 min. per side; transfer to a plate.

3. Add asparagus to skillet and cook, stirring occasionally, 3 min.; toss with scallions. Add wine and simmer 2 min., then stir in mustard.

4. Nestle pork among asparagus mixture and continue cooking until just cooked through, 2 to 4 min. more.

KITCHEN TIP *When slicing asparagus, keep the spears rubber-banded together. Use a chef's knife to chop off ends with one quick cut, then snip bands.*

PESTO CHICKEN & GREEN BEANS

The cherry tomatoes crinkle and burst in the oven, creating a sauce-like mixture to coat the tender beans.

1	Tbsp olive oil
8	small chicken thighs (about 2 lbs total)
	Kosher salt and pepper
8	oz green beans, halved
1	cup cherry tomatoes
1	15-oz can butter beans, rinsed
2	Tbsp pesto
	Grated Parmesan and chopped basil, for serving

Active time: 25 min.

Total time: 25 min.

Serves: 4

About 450 cal
26 g fat (6.5 g sat)
38 g pro
770 mg sodium
22 g carb
6 g fiber

1. Heat oven to 425°F. Heat oil in large oven-safe skillet on medium-high. Season chicken with ½ tsp each salt and pepper and cook, skin-side down, until golden brown, about 6 min.

2. Turn chicken, scatter green beans, tomatoes and beans around, season them with ¼ tsp each salt and pepper and roast until chicken is cooked through (165°F), 12 to 15 min.

3. Brush pesto over chicken and serve sprinkled with grated Parmesan and basil, if desired.

BACON & EGG FRIED RICE

Here's a great idea for leftover rice—add bacon and eggs
for a tasty twist on breakfast for dinner!

1	**Tbsp canola oil**
5	**slices bacon, chopped**
1	**bunch scallions, sliced**
1	**cup frozen peas, thawed**
3	**cups cooked leftover white rice**
1	**5-oz bag baby spinach**
	Kosher salt
4	**fried eggs**

Active time: 10 min.

Total time: 15 min.

Serves: 4

About 485 cal
24 g fat (7 g sat)
17 g pro
575 mg sodium
47 g carb
3 g fiber

1. Heat oil in large skillet on medium-high. Add bacon and cook, stirring often, until crisp. Add scallions and peas and cook, tossing, 2 min.

2. Add rice and cook, tossing occasionally, 3 min. Add spinach, season with ½ tsp salt and cook, tossing until beginning to wilt, 2 to 3 min. Transfer to plates and top with fried eggs.

SHRIMP LINGUINE PUTTANESCA

A fast meal that doesn't skimp on flavor: Olives, garlic, capers and tomatoes will keep everyone coming back for seconds.

2	**Tbsp olive oil**
¼	**cup pitted kalamata olives**
2	**cloves garlic, chopped**
1	**Tbsp capers, rinsed**
4	**cups low-sodium chicken broth**
1	**cup marinara sauce**
12	**oz linguine**
1	**lb medium peeled and deveined shrimp**
8	**oz plum tomatoes, roughly chopped**
½	**cup fresh basil leaves, torn**
	Black pepper

Active time: 10 min.

Total time: 20 min.

Serves: 4

About 555 cal
13.5 g fat (2.5 g sat)
34 g pro
1,200 mg sodium
76 g carb
5 g fiber

1. Heat oil, olives, garlic and capers in large deep skillet on medium until garlic is light golden brown, about 2 min. Remove from heat and mix in broth and marinara sauce.

2. Add linguine and bring to a boil. Reduce heat and simmer, stirring often, 10 min.

3. Nestle shrimp in mixture and cook until opaque throughout, 3 to 4 min. Fold in tomatoes, basil and ½ tsp pepper.

KITCHEN TIP *Try using a larger than usual skillet (preferably bigger than the recommended 12-in. one) so the pasta can lie flat and cook evenly.*

GET MORE CHICKEN FOR LESS $$$

Here's how to save money by turning boneless chicken breast halves into cutlets.

1. Place a boneless, skinless chicken breast half on a cutting board. Hold it flat with the palm of one hand; with a chef's knife, carefully slice the breast in half horizontally.

2. Open the breast like a book; make a cut to separate the two halves if necessary.

3. Place one hand over the other; use the heel of the bottom hand to press down and flatten each piece of chicken into a ½-in.-thick cutlet.

MOROCCAN OLIVE & ORANGE CHICKEN

Our twist on this traditionally slow-simmered chicken dish is ready in just 20 minutes.

¼	cup all-purpose flour
4	4-oz boneless, skinless chicken breast cutlets
	Kosher salt and pepper
3	Tbsp olive oil
1	small red onion, sliced
2	navel oranges
½	cup pitted green olives, halved
	Rice pilaf and chopped parsley, for serving

Active time: 10 min.

Total time: 20 min.

Serves: 4

About 440 cal
18 g fat (3 g sat)
31 g pro
790 mg sodium
40 g carb
3 g fiber

1. Spread flour on a sheet of waxed paper. Season chicken with ¼ tsp each salt and pepper, then coat in flour.

2. Heat oil in large skillet on medium-high and cook chicken until browned, 3 min. per side; transfer to plate.

3. Reduce heat to medium; cook onion, stirring occasionally, 3 min. Squeeze juice from 1½ oranges into skillet. Thinly slice remaining ½ orange, add to skillet along with olives and ¼ cup water; bring to a simmer.

4. Return chicken to skillet and cook until just cooked through, about 3 min. Serve over rice and sprinkle with parsley.

SEARED STEAK WITH BLISTERED TOMATOES

The blue cheese vinaigrette alone is enough of a reason to
pull out the skillet for this speedy supper.

2	1¹/₂-in.-thick strip steaks (about 1¹/₂ lbs)
	Kosher salt and pepper
4	Tbsp olive oil, divided
6	cloves garlic, in their skins
2	bunches cherry tomatoes on the vine (about 1¹/₂ lbs)
2	sprigs fresh rosemary
2	Tbsp white wine vinegar
¹/₄	small red onion, finely chopped
3	Tbsp crumbled blue cheese (about 1 oz)
	Arugula salad, for serving

Active time: 20 min.

Total time: 20 min.

Serves: 4

About 445 cal
28 g fat (8.5 g sat)
39 g pro
455 mg sodium
9 g carb
2 g fiber

1. Heat oven to 450°F. Heat large oven-safe skillet on medium-
high. Season steaks with salt and pepper. Add 1 tsp oil to
skillet, then add steaks and garlic and cook until steaks are
browned, 3 min. per side.

2. Place tomatoes on the vine and rosemary in skillet, drizzle
with 2 tsp oil and season with salt and pepper. Transfer skillet
to oven and roast until steak is at desired doneness and
tomatoes begin to slightly break down, 3 to 4 min. for medium-
rare. Transfer steaks to cutting board and let rest at least 5 min.
before serving. Transfer tomatoes and garlic to platter;
squeeze garlic cloves from skins.

3. In small bowl, combine vinegar, remaining 3 Tbsp oil and
¹/₄ tsp each salt and pepper; stir in onion and fold in blue
cheese. Serve steak, tomatoes and garlic drizzled with
vinaigrette, and arugula salad.

LEMON CHICKEN & PEA GEMELLI

Yep—the chicken and pasta are cooked in the same skillet for a truly one-pan dinner.

2	Tbsp olive oil
12	oz boneless, skinless chicken breasts, cut into 2-in. pieces
¼	cup lemon juice, plus 2 tsp finely grated lemon zest
	Kosher salt and pepper
4	cups low-sodium chicken broth
12	oz gemelli or other short pasta
4	oz cream cheese, at room temperature
1	cup peas, thawed if frozen
½	cup finely grated Parmesan
1	Tbsp finely chopped tarragon

Active time: 20 min.

Total time: 25 min.

Serves: 4

About 675 cal
23.5 g fat (9 g sat)
41 g pro
535 mg sodium
75 g carb
5 g fiber

1. Heat oil in large deep skillet on medium-high. Season chicken with ¼ tsp each salt and pepper and cook until golden brown on all sides, 4 to 5 min.; transfer to large bowl. Add lemon juice to pan, scraping up any brown bits, then pour over chicken in bowl.

2. Add broth and pasta to skillet and bring to a boil. Reduce heat and simmer, stirring often, for 10 min.

3. Return chicken (and any juices) to skillet and continue to cook until pasta is just tender, about 3 min.

4. Add cream cheese, stirring to melt, then fold in peas, lemon zest, Parmesan and tarragon.

TORTELLINI & LEMONY SNOW PEAS

Get your greens in with this comforting cheese tortellini in a flavor-spiked basil pesto broth.

4	cups low-sodium vegetable or chicken broth
1	lb fresh cheese tortellini
6	oz snow peas, trimmed and halved diagonally
2	Tbsp basil pesto
	Zest of 1 lemon
¼	cup grated Parmesan, plus more for serving

Active time: 10 min.

Total time: 15 min.

Serves: 4

About 460 cal
14.5 g fat (6 g sat)
24 g pro
690 mg sodium
61 g carb
4 g fiber

1. Bring broth to a simmer in large skillet. Add tortellini and simmer until barely tender, 4 to 5 min., per pkg. directions.

2. Add snow peas and simmer until tortellini and snow peas are tender, 1 to 2 min. Remove from heat and stir in pesto, then gently toss with lemon zest and Parmesan. Serve with additional Parmesan, if desired.

KITCHEN TIP *No need to drain! This one-pot pasta is cooked in broth, which makes for a flavorful finished sauce without any extra ingredients.*

STEWED PEPPERS & TOMATOES WITH EGGS

Dunk a piece of warm toast into savory, saucy tomatoes and poached eggs
for a cozy meal that's perfect for breakfast, dinner or brunch.

2	Tbsp olive oil
1	medium onion, chopped
2	bell peppers (red and orange), quartered lengthwise, then sliced crosswise
	Kosher salt and pepper
4	cloves garlic, finely chopped
1	28-oz can whole tomatoes in juice
8	large eggs
	Chopped cilantro, for serving
4	slices toasted bread

Active time: 20 min.

Total time: 30 min.

Serves: 4

About 345 cal
17.5 g fat (4 g sat)
19 g pro
910 mg sodium
28 g carb
5 g fiber

1. Heat oil in large skillet on medium. Add onion and cook, covered, 4 min. Add bell peppers, season with ½ tsp each salt and pepper, and cook, covered, stirring occasionally, until just tender, 6 to 8 min. Stir in garlic and cook 1 min.

2. Crush tomatoes with your hands and add to skillet along with their juices. Bring to a boil, then reduce heat and simmer until mixture has slightly thickened, about 5 min.

3. Make 8 small wells in sauce and carefully crack an egg into each one. Cover and gently simmer 6 min. Uncover and cook until whites are set and yolks are cooked to desired doneness, 6 to 7 min. for slightly runny yolks. Sprinkle with chopped cilantro, if desired, and serve with toast.

INDIAN-SPICED RICE WITH SHRIMP & PEAS

Fresh ginger, garlic and curry powder make this colorful dinner
taste as good as your kitchen will smell.

1	Tbsp olive oil
1	large onion, finely chopped
	Kosher salt and pepper
1½	Tbsp grated peeled fresh ginger
2	cloves garlic, finely chopped
1	Tbsp curry powder
1	cup long-grain white rice
1	lb medium peeled and deveined shrimp
1	cup frozen peas, thawed
1	cup fresh cilantro, chopped
	Lemon wedges, for serving

Active time: 20 min.

Total time: 30 min.

Serves: 4

About 345 cal
5.5 g fat (1 g sat)
22 g pro
790 mg sodium
51 g carb
4 g fiber

1. Heat oil in large skillet on medium. Add onion, season with
¼ tsp each salt and pepper, and cook, covered, stirring
occasionally, until tender, 6 to 8 min. Add ginger and garlic and
cook, stirring, 2 min. Add curry powder and cook, stirring, 1 min.

2. Add rice and stir to coat in onion mixture. Stir in 2 cups water
and bring to a boil. Reduce heat and simmer, covered, 15 min.

3. Fold shrimp and peas into rice and cook, covered, until shrimp
are opaque throughout and rice is tender, 4 to 5 min. more.

4. Remove from heat and fold in cilantro. Serve with lemon
wedges, if desired.

KITCHEN TIP *Check the label: The main ingredient in many curry powders is turmeric, which has a bold color but not a bold flavor. Look for curry powders that list coriander or cumin first instead.*

ONE-PAN SPRING CHICKEN WITH ASPARAGUS & EDAMAME

Dill, sour cream and lemon stirred in at the end create
a winning weeknight chicken dinner.

3	Tbsp all-purpose flour
	Kosher salt and pepper
4	6-oz boneless, skinless chicken breasts
2	Tbsp olive oil
1	small red onion, thinly sliced
1	clove garlic, finely chopped
½	cup dry white wine
1	cup low-sodium chicken broth
1	lb medium asparagus, sliced ¼-in. thick on a diagonal
1	cup frozen edamame, thawed
2	Tbsp fresh dill, chopped
1	Tbsp sour cream
1	Tbsp fresh lemon juice
	Steamed new potatoes or crusty bread, for serving

Active time: 20 min.

Total time: 30 min.

Serves: 4

About 360 cal
14 g fat (2.5 g sat)
44 g pro
475 mg sodium
15 g carb
4 g fiber

1. In shallow bowl, whisk together flour and ½ tsp each salt and pepper. Coat chicken breasts in flour mixture.

2. Heat oil in large skillet on medium heat and cook chicken breasts until golden brown on one side, 4 to 6 min. Turn chicken, add onion and garlic and cook, stirring onion and garlic occasionally, 3 min.

3. Add wine to skillet and simmer, scraping up any browned bits, until reduced by half, 1 to 2 min. Add broth, return to a boil, then reduce and simmer until chicken is cooked through, 5 to 6 min. more.

4. Two min. before chicken is done, add asparagus and edamame to skillet and cook, stirring occasionally, until just tender.

5. Remove from heat and stir in dill, sour cream and lemon juice. Serve with potatoes or crusty bread, if desired.

KITCHEN TIP *Substitute 4 small boneless pork chops for the chicken. Cook until golden brown on one side, 3 to 4 min., then turn, add the onion and garlic and cook as directed.*

ORECCHIETTE WITH WHITE BEANS & SPINACH

Cooking the orecchiette in vegetable bouillon lends instant flavor to a near-instant dinner. You'll have this combo of creamy white beans, spinach and pasta ready in 20 minutes.

2	Tbsp olive oil
4	cloves garlic, finely chopped
2	tsp vegetable bouillon base (we used Better Than Bouillon)
12	oz orecchiette or other short pasta
2	tsp fresh thyme leaves
1	can small white beans, rinsed
2	cups baby spinach
½	cup finely grated Parmesan
	Black pepper

Active time: 15 min.

Total time: 20 min.

Serves: 4

About 500 cal
11.5 g fat (2.5 g sat)
21 g pro
675 mg sodium
84 g carb
8 g fiber

1. Heat oil and garlic in large deep skillet on medium until garlic is light golden brown, about 2 min. Remove from heat, add 4 cups water and whisk in bouillon base.

2. Add orecchiette and thyme and bring to a boil. Reduce heat and simmer, stirring frequently, until orecchiette is firm-tender, 10 to 12 min.

3. Fold in beans, spinach, Parmesan and ½ tsp pepper and cook until beans are heated through, about 2 min.

Garlic Wings, Two Ways, recipe on p 77

2

THE MIGHTY MULTI-COOKER

Cooking dinner in an instant sounds too good to be true until you do so in a multi-cooker. A multi-cooker is great for two solid reasons: saving time and space in the kitchen. This go-to kitchen appliance replaces all the other clunky ones by working as a pressure cooker, slow cooker, rice cooker, steamer and more.

MULTI-COOKER MUST-HAVES

Narrowing down the best multi-cooker for your everyday cooking needs can be a breeze with this short checklist.

- **DESIRED FUNCTIONS.** Multi-cookers can also brown, pressure cook, slow cook, and even air fry to name a few capabilities—which also go hand-in-hand with price. Consider your needs when comparing models.
- **SEARING ABILITY.** Browning food before cooking adds flavor to the final product. Some multi-cookers have different temperature levels so you can lightly sweat vegetables or sear meat.

✅ **SIZE.** Six quarts is common, but smaller and larger exist. Consider counter space, storing, and recipe sizes when shopping. Small cookers are ideal for one to two people, but the largest ones are best for families or stocking up on broth.

✅ **SHAPE.** Round multi-cookers are common, but oblong and rectangular cooking pots better accommodate large roasts.

COOKING PROGRAM OPTIONS

Depending on which multi-cooker you're using, there are a variety of pre-programmed buttons for easy use. These are the most common programs.

NOTE: Be sure to check with the manufacturer's instructions for specific operating instructions for your multi-cooker.

PROGRAM	MODE	COOKING OPTION
Bean & Chili	Less	Less soft texture
	Normal	Soft texture
	More	Very soft texture
Egg	Less	Soft-boiled egg
	Normal	Medium-boiled egg
	More	Hard-boiled egg
Meat & Stew	Less	Use for soft meat texture
	Normal	Use for very soft meat texture
	More	Use for fall-off-the-bone meat texture
Multigrain	Less	Wild rice, brown rice, mung beans, etc.
	Normal	Wild rice, brown rice, mung beans, etc.
	More	Tough grains or a mixture of grains and beans
Rice	Less	Al dente white rice
	Normal	Normal texture white rice
	More	Softer texture white rice

PROGRAM	MODE	COOKING OPTION
Sauté	Less	Simmering, thickening and reducing liquids
	Normal	Pan searing or sautéing
	More	Stir-frying or browning
Slow Cook	Less	Corresponds to LOW setting in a temperature-controlled slow cooker
	Normal	Corresponds to MEDIUM setting in a temperature-controlled slow cooker
	More	Corresponds to HIGH setting in a temperature-controlled slow cooker
Soup & Broth	Less	Use for soup without meat
	Normal	Use for soup with meat
	More	Use for rich bone broth
Steam	Less	Use for vegetables
	Normal	Use for fish and seafood
	More	Use for meat

For recipes in this section, your multi-cooker will act as a pressure cooker for the most part. It drastically reduces cook time by raising the boiling point of water and trapping steam, making it great for tenderizing meat in half the time it normally takes.

TWO WAYS OF RELEASING PRESSURE

As a rule of thumb, natural release is best for stews and other foods that won't overcook, while quick release is best for dishes like pasta that are at risk of overcooking. Here are some tips on how to perform both.

QUICK RELEASE: Use tongs (instead of your bare hands) to turn the steam release handle to the Venting position to let steam out until the float valve drops down. Never pull out the steam release handle while releasing steam as escaping steam is extremely hot and can cause scalds. For food with large liquid volume or starch content, use Natural Release instead as thick liquid may splatter out.

NATURAL RELEASE: Allow the cooker to cool down naturally until the float valve drops down. This may take 10 to 40 min., or even more, depending on the amount of food in the cooker. Place a wet towel on the lid to speed up cooling.

MULTI-COOKER SAFETY TIPS

While pressure cookers of the past might have been dicey safety-wise, most multi-cookers have plenty of safety mechanisms built in so that you don't need to worry about them being dangerous.

The silicone gasket prevents steam from escaping and helps regulate pressure, while a floating valve acts as an indicator that pops up when it's unsafe to open the lid while cooking foods. As an added safety measure, most multi-cookers will automatically lock the lid in place when the floating valve is raised. Still, when pressure cooking in a multi-cooker, there are important safety tips to keep in mind.

- Do not open the multi-cooker until it has cooled and all internal pressure has been released. If the float valve is still up or the lid is difficult to turn, it is an indication that the cooker is still pressurized. Do not force it open.

- Make sure the steam release valve is in the Sealing position for all the pressure-cooking programs.

- Always check the steam release valve, float valve and anti-block shield for clogging before use.

- For all pressure-cooking programs, the total amount of precooked food and liquid in the inner pot should not pass the ⅔ line. When cooking food that expands during cooking such as rice, beans or vegetables, the inner pot should not pass the ½ line.

- Be aware that certain foods, such as applesauce, cranberries, pearl barley, oatmeal and other cereals, split peas, noodles, macaroni, rhubarb and spaghetti can foam, froth, sputter and clog the steam release. We do not recommend cooking these dishes under pressure, but they can be made using other functions like on Slow Cook.

MULTI-COOKER RECIPES

GARLIC LEMON CHICKEN WITH BROCCOLI RICE

With help from your trusty multi-cooker, you can crisp chicken thighs and perfectly steam rice and broccoli. And you'll only have one dish to do after dinner.

6	cloves garlic, 2 finely grated and 4 thinly sliced
	Pinch cayenne
3	Tbsp olive oil, divided
	Kosher salt and pepper
4	chicken thighs (about 1 lb), trimmed and patted dry
1	medium onion, chopped
1	cup long-grain white rice
1	lemon, thinly sliced, plus wedges for serving
1	small broccoli crown, finely chopped (about 2 cups)

Active time: 30 min.

Pressure time: 5 min.

Total time: 30 min.

Pressure level: High

Release: Quick

Serves: 4

About 625 cal
34 g fat (8 g sat)
29 g pro
490 mg sodium
48 g carb
2 g fiber

1. In large bowl, combine grated garlic, cayenne, 1 Tbsp oil, and ½ tsp each salt and pepper. Add chicken and toss to coat.

2. Press Sauté on multi-cooker, adjust to Medium and heat remaining 2 Tbsp oil. Place chicken, skin-side down, in single layer and cook until golden brown, 4 min. per side. Transfer to plate.

3. Add onion and cook, stirring occasionally, 3 min. Stir in sliced garlic and cook 1 min. Press Cancel. Stir in rice, 1¼ cups water and ¼ tsp salt and stir to scrape up any browned bits.

4. Place steam rack on top of rice, then lay lemon slices in single layer on rack. Place chicken on top of lemons, skin-side up. Lock lid and cook on High pressure (12.0) 5 min. Use quick pressure release and remove lid carefully.

5. Lift steam rack out of pressure cooker and fluff rice with fork. Fold in broccoli, lay clean kitchen towel across top, then replace lid and let it sit 5 min. Serve chicken alongside rice with lemon wedges, if desired.

ASIAN NOODLES & MEATBALLS

Garlic-ginger pork meatballs in a super simple peanut sauce is the one-pot wonder your next weeknight dinner needs.

1	lb ground pork
¼	cup panko
1	large egg
4	scallions, finely chopped, white and green parts separated
½	cup cilantro, finely chopped
4	tsp finely grated fresh ginger, divided
2	large cloves garlic, finely grated, divided
	Kosher salt and pepper
8	oz linguine, broken in half
2	Tbsp toasted sesame oil, divided
3	Tbsp creamy peanut butter
1½	Tbsp low-sodium soy sauce
1	Tbsp fresh lime juice, plus lime wedges for serving
1	tsp light brown sugar
	Thinly sliced red chile and sesame seeds, for serving

Active time: 30 min.

Pressure time: 6 min.

Total time: 30 min.

Pressure level: High

Release: Quick

Serves: 4

About 535 cal
20 g fat (4.5 g sat)
38 g pro
735 mg sodium
53 g carb
3 g fiber

1. In large bowl, combine pork, panko, egg, scallion whites, cilantro, half of ginger, two-thirds of garlic, and ½ tsp each salt and pepper. Form into 1½-in. balls (you should have about 16).

2. In pot of multi-cooker, stir together noodles and 1 Tbsp oil to coat. Place meatballs on top of noodles, pour in 1¾ cups water, and add ¼ tsp salt. Lock lid and cook on High pressure (12.0) 6 min. Use quick pressure release and remove lid carefully.

3. Meanwhile, in medium bowl, whisk together peanut butter, soy sauce, lime juice, brown sugar, and remaining sesame oil, ginger and garlic.

4. Stir peanut sauce into noodles and cover with lid. Let sit 5 min. then transfer noodles and meatballs to serving plates.

5. Top with scallion greens, red chile and sesame seeds and serve with lime wedges for squeezing.

NO-STIR CREAMY PARMESAN RISOTTO

The multi-cooker makes this typically fussy Italian dish
easier than ever but just as flavorful.

1	**Tbsp unsalted butter**
1	**Tbsp olive oil**
1	**medium onion, finely chopped**
2	**cloves garlic, finely chopped**
1½	**cups Arborio rice**
	Kosher salt and pepper
½	**cup dry white wine**
3½	**cups low-sodium chicken broth**
½	**cup freshly grated Parmesan, plus more for serving**

Active time: 15 min.

Pressure time: 5 min.

Total time: 30 min.

Pressure level: High

Release: Quick

Serves: 4

About 405 cal
11 g fat (4 g sat)
14 g pro
725 mg sodium
65 g carb
4 g fiber

1. Press Sauté on multi-cooker, adjust to Medium and heat
butter and oil with onion, then cook, stirring occasionally, until
tender, 6 min. Stir in garlic and cook 2 min.

2. Stir in rice and 1 tsp salt and cook, stirring occasionally, until
golden brown and toasted, 4 to 6 min. Add wine and cook until
absorbed, about 1 min. Stir in broth, then press Cancel.

3. Lock lid and cook on High pressure (12.0) 5 min. Use quick-
release method to release pressure, then open lid. Stir risotto
until liquid has been absorbed, 2 to 3 min. Stir in Parmesan.
Serve with additional Parmesan and cracked pepper, if desired.

KITCHEN TIP *Just before serving, stir in preferred flavorings and dress
with toppings.*
- *¼ cup prepared pesto and top with a fried egg*
- *2 cups baby spinach + 2 scallions (thinly sliced)*
- *1 tsp lemon zest + ¾ cup frozen peas (thawed) + 1 cup pea shoots*

SUPER-FAST VEGGIE CHILI

Canned beans, frozen corn and plenty of spice help get this hearty and flavor-packed vegetarian dinner on the table in 20 minutes.

1	**Tbsp olive oil**
3	**cloves garlic, finely chopped**
12	**scallions, white and green parts chopped, with 2 Tbsp chopped greens reserved**
1	**bell pepper, any color, diced**
1	**jalapeño, finely chopped**
1	**tsp ground cumin**
2	**tsp chili powder**
	Kosher salt and pepper
2	**15-oz cans black beans, rinsed**
1	**15-oz can pinto or kidney beans, rinsed**
1	**14.5-oz can diced tomatoes**
1	**cup frozen corn**
½	**cup lager beer or water**
	Sour cream and tortilla chips, for serving

Active time: 5 min.

Pressure time: 3 min.

Total time: 20 min.

Pressure level: High

Release: Quick

Serves: 4

About 410 cal
1 g fat (1 g sat)
21 g pro
660 mg sodium
67 g carb
20 g fiber

1. Press Sauté on multi-cooker, adjust to Medium and heat oil. Add garlic, scallions, bell pepper and jalapeño and cook, stirring until vegetables begin to soften, 3 to 4 min.

2. Stir in cumin, chili powder, ½ tsp salt and ¼ tsp pepper and cook, stirring, for 1 min.

3. Add beans, tomatoes with juice, corn and beer. Press Cancel.

4. Lock lid and cook on High pressure (12.0) 3 min. Use quick-release method to release pressure, then open lid and stir. (If you prefer thicker chili, select Sauté and adjust to More for high heat and simmer to desired consistency.) Serve sprinkled with reserved scallions, a dollop of sour cream and chips, if using.

KITCHEN TIP *Not a fan of black beans? Switch it out to your liking—white beans and chickpeas work really well here too.*

ALOO GOBI

The secret to packing serious flavor into this simple cauliflower
and potato dish: Add dry spices, like cumin, coriander and garam masala
at the beginning to ensure they toast.

1	Tbsp peanut oil
1	tsp cumin seeds
1	large russet potato, cut into 1/2-in. pieces (about 2 cups)
1	tsp garam masala
1/2	tsp ground turmeric
1/4	tsp ground cumin
1/2	tsp ground coriander
1/4	tsp cayenne
	Kosher salt
1	large tomato, cut into 1/2-in. pieces
1	small head cauliflower, cored and cut into large florets
1/4	cup fresh cilantro, chopped
	Warm naan, for serving

Active time: 26 min.

Pressure time: 3 min.

Total time: 30 min.

Pressure level: Low

Release: Quick

Serves: 4

About 90 cal
4 g fat (0.5 g sat)
3 g pro
615 mg sodium
13 g carb
4 g fiber

1. Press Sauté on multi-cooker and adjust to High. Add oil and heat until it shimmers. Add cumin seeds and stir. Cook until they begin to sputter.

2. Add potato and cook, stirring occasionally until it begins to brown, 3 min. Add garam masala, turmeric, cumin, coriander and cayenne and 1/2 tsp salt and cook, stirring, 1 min.

3. Add tomato and 1/4 cup water and cook, stirring, scraping up any browned bits. Gently stir in cauliflower and press Cancel. Lock lid and cook on Low pressure 3 min.

4. Use quick-release method to release pressure, then carefully open lid. Sprinkle with cilantro and serve with naan, if desired.

QUINOA TABBOULEH

Lots of lemon, fresh herbs, crunchy cucumber and juicy tomatoes take
this protein-rich grain from bland to brilliant.

1	**cup quinoa, rinsed and drained**
2	**Tbsp olive oil, divided**
	Kosher salt and pepper
1	**medium tomato, seeded and finely chopped**
1	**small cucumber, finely chopped**
1	**large clove garlic, finely chopped**
1/3	**cup finely chopped fresh mint or parsley, or a combination**
	Juice of 1 lemon

Active time: 5 min.

Pressure time: 1 min.

Total time: 20 min.

Pressure level: Low

Release: Natural

Serves: 4 to 6

About 255 cal
1 g fat (1 g sat)
8 g pro
295 mg sodium
35 g carb
4 g fiber

1. In multi-cooker, combine quinoa, 1²/₃ cups water, 1 Tbsp
olive oil and ½ tsp salt. Lock lid and cook on Low pressure
1 min.

2. Let pressure release naturally, then transfer quinoa to large
bowl and let cool briefly.

3. Stir in tomato, cucumber, garlic, mint or parsley, remaining
1 Tbsp olive oil and lemon juice. Taste and season with ¼ tsp
each salt and pepper.

SPICY TOFU CURRY WITH RICE

Tofu is the perfect canvas for building a lot of flavor, and Thai red curry paste, chile and scallions really bring the heat.

1	Tbsp extra virgin olive oil
1	medium onion, chopped
3	cloves garlic, finely chopped
1	small red bell pepper, seeded and chopped
	Kosher salt and pepper
2	Tbsp tomato paste
3/4	cup low-sodium vegetable broth
1	14-oz can diced tomatoes, drained
1	Tbsp fresh lime juice
1	tsp Thai red curry paste
1	tsp curry powder
1	tsp sugar
1	lb firm or extra-firm tofu, drained and cut into 1-in. cubes
2	cups cooked white rice
2	scallions, sliced
1	red chile, thinly sliced

Active time: 15 min.

Pressure time: 4 min.

Total time: 25 min.

Pressure level: High

Release: Quick

Serves: 4

About 325 cal
11 g fat (1.5 g sat)
17 g pro
525 mg sodium
43 g carb
4 g fiber

1. Press Sauté on multi-cooker, adjust to High and heat oil. Add onion, garlic and bell pepper, season with ¼ tsp salt and cook, stirring often until beginning to soften, about 3 min.

2. Stir in tomato paste and then broth and tomatoes. Stir in lime juice, curry paste, curry powder and sugar. Lock lid and cook on High pressure (12.0) 4 min.

3. Use quick-release method to release pressure, then carefully open lid. Let sit for 2 min., then serve over rice topped with scallions and chile.

CHICKEN & BISCUITS

A bowl of this stew packs in the flavor of chicken pot pie without all of the fuss.

1/4	cup all-purpose flour
1/8	tsp cayenne
	Kosher salt and pepper
1 1/4	lbs boneless, skinless chicken thighs or breasts
4	Tbsp unsalted butter
3	cups chicken broth, plus more as needed
3	large carrots, cut into 1-in. half-moons
2	large celery stalks, chopped
1	cup frozen pearl onions
1	cup frozen peas, thawed
	Biscuits (recipe at right)

Active time: 20 min.

Pressure time: 5 min.

Total time: 30 min.

Pressure level: High

Release: Quick

Serves: 4

About 705 cal
31 g fat (20 g sat)
50 g pro
1,135 mg sodium
54 g carb
5 g fiber

1. In shallow dish, stir together flour, cayenne, 1/2 tsp salt and 1/8 tsp pepper. Coat chicken thighs in seasoned flour, shaking off any excess. Reserve remaining flour mixture to use again in step 3.

2. Press Sauté on multi-cooker; adjust to High and melt butter. When foam subsides, working in 2 batches, cook chicken until golden brown, 2 to 3 min. per side. Transfer chicken to plate and let cool briefly. Cut into pieces.

3. With multi-cooker still on Sauté, add remaining flour mixture to butter and cook, stirring constantly, until roux is golden brown. Whisk in 1 cup broth, to combine with roux, then whisk in remaining 2 cups broth, scraping up any browned bits from bottom. Simmer until sauce thickens slightly. If sauce is very thick, add more chicken broth until consistency is like light gravy.

4. Add chicken, carrots, celery and onions to pot. Lock lid and cook on High pressure (12.0) 5 min.

5. Use quick-release method to release pressure, then carefully remove lid. Stir in peas and heat through, 2 min. Spoon chicken mixture into shallow bowls. Top with biscuits.

BISCUITS

Heat oven to 400°F. In bowl, whisk 1½ cups self-rising flour and ¾ cup heavy whipping cream until mixture holds together. Scoop by ¼-cupfuls onto lined baking sheet. Bake until golden brown, 14 to 16 min.

PARMESAN TURKEY MEATBALLS

Juicy meatballs turn even the simplest pasta dish into a hearty main.
Make a double batch to freeze so you'll always have them on hand.

1	large egg
2	Tbsp whole milk
¼	cup breadcrumbs
1	lb ground turkey
½	medium onion, finely chopped
3	cloves garlic, finely chopped
2	Tbsp finely chopped fresh parsley
½	cup grated Parmesan cheese
	Kosher salt
2	Tbsp olive oil
½	cup low-sodium chicken broth
1	14-oz can diced tomatoes
	Chopped parsley, for garnish
1	lb cooked penne, for serving (optional)

Active time: 15 min.

Pressure time: 5 min.

Total time: 30 min.

Pressure level: High

Release: Natural and Quick

Serves: 4

About 405 cal
25 g fat (6 g sat)
40 g pro
715 mg sodium
12 g carb
2 g fiber

1. In large bowl, whisk together egg and milk, then stir in breadcrumbs. Add turkey, onion, garlic, parsley, Parmesan and ½ tsp salt and gently mix to combine. With moistened hands, form meatballs, using about 2 Tbsp meat for each.

2. Press Sauté on multi-cooker; adjust to High and heat oil. Add meatballs in single layer and brown, 1 to 2 min. per side. Move meatballs to side of multi-cooker, stacking as needed, and add chicken broth and cook, scraping up any browned bits from the bottom.

3. Add tomatoes with their juices and move meatballs back into an even layer. Lock lid and cook on High pressure (12.0) 5 min.

4. Let pressure release naturally 5 min., then release any remaining pressure. Carefully remove lid and using slotted spoon, transfer meatballs to bowl.

5. Press Sauté and adjust to High heat and simmer until sauce thickens. Spoon sauce over meatballs and serve on top of penne and sprinkle with parsley.

GARLIC WINGS, TWO WAYS

Double the glaze and save half to serve with the wings
for extra game-time dipping.

12	whole chicken wings, split

TO MAKE GINGER-SOY GLAZE

1/3	cup honey
1/4	cup soy sauce
1	Tbsp grated fresh ginger
4	cloves garlic, finely chopped
1	tsp toasted sesame oil

TO MAKE HONEY-MUSTARD GLAZE

1/3	cup honey
1/3	cup Dijon mustard
4	cloves garlic, finely chopped

Active time: 15 min.

Pressure time: 10 min.

Total time: 30 min.

Pressure level: High

Release: Quick

Serves: 4

About 350 cal
18 g fat (7 g sat)
20 g pro
65 mg sodium
29 g carb
2 g fiber

1. Line rimmed baking sheet with foil and place wire rack on top; set aside. Remove wing tips and save for another use.

2. Put steamer basket into multi-cooker and pour in 1 cup water. Place chicken wings in steamer basket. Lock lid and cook on High pressure (12.0) 10 min.

3. Use quick-release method to release pressure, then carefully open lid. Transfer wings to wire rack and heat broiler.

4. In small bowl, stir together glaze ingredients. Baste wings with half of glaze. Broil wings until browned, 4 to 6 min. Flip and baste wings with remaining glaze. Broil until second side is browned, 3 to 6 min.

CHICKEN SOUP

Soup's up! In 30 minutes, you can prep and cook a comforting classic, full of carrots, celery and plenty of noodles, that puts any can to shame.

1	**3- to 3½-lb chicken, including neck (discard giblets), skin removed**
2	**large carrots, halved**
2	**stalks celery, halved, plus celery leaves, for serving**
1	**onion, quartered**
1	**clove garlic, smashed**
1	**bay leaf**
4	**sprigs parsley**
	Kosher salt
1½	**cups egg noodles**
	Chopped dill, for serving

Active time: 15 min.
Pressure time: 15 min.
Total time: 30 min.
Pressure level: High
Release: Quick
Serves: 6

About 305 cal
16 g fat (4.5 g sat)
28 g pro
345 mg sodium
11 g carb
2 g fiber

1. Place chicken in multi-cooker and add carrots, celery, onion, garlic, bay leaf, parsley, ¾ tsp salt and 6 cups water. Lock lid and cook on High pressure (12.0) 15 min. Use quick pressure release and carefully remove lid. Transfer chicken to bowl and carrots and celery to cutting board; let cool.

2. Strain broth in pot through fine-mesh sieve, discarding any remaining solids; transfer back to pot, press Sauté and bring mixture to a simmer. Add noodles and cook until tender, 5 to 6 min. Press Cancel.

3. Meanwhile, cut carrots and celery into small chunks and shred chicken into large pieces, discarding skin and bones. Stir into broth and serve soup sprinkled with dill and celery leaves if desired.

ONE-POT PASTA BOLOGNESE

This traditional Italian dish is on the table in half the time it would normally take. Bonus: Clean-up is quicker too.

1	Tbsp olive oil
12	oz lean ground beef
1	large onion, chopped
3	cloves garlic, finely chopped
½	cup dry red wine
¼	tsp red pepper flakes
	Kosher salt
12	oz ziti
1	28-oz can crushed tomatoes in purée, or good tomato sauce
½	cup coarsely grated mozzarella cheese

Active time: 10 min.
Pressure time: 5 min.
Total time: 30 min.
Pressure level: High
Release: Quick
Serves: 4

About 595 cal
4 g fat (6 g sat)
45 g pro
840 mg sodium
68 g carb
7 g fiber

1. Press Sauté on multi-cooker; adjust to High and heat oil. Add beef and cook, breaking it up until no longer pink and beginning to brown, 3 min.

2. Add onion. Cook, stirring, 1 min. Add garlic. Cook 1 min. more.

3. Add wine and cook, scraping up any browned bits from bottom of multi-cooker, 2 min. Stir in red pepper flakes, ½ tsp salt and 1½ cups water and then pasta.

4. Pour tomatoes over in even layer, covering pasta. Lock lid and cook on High pressure (12.0) 5 min.

5. Use quick-release method to release pressure, then carefully remove lid. Test pasta. If not quite done, select Sauté and simmer 1 to 2 min. more. Serve topped with mozzarella.

SPICY BEEF WITH VEGETABLES

Thinly sliced beef soaks up all the flavors of the sweet and spicy garlic-ginger sauce.

3	Tbsp vegetable oil, divided
2	12- to 14-oz top sirloin steaks, about 1-in. thick
	Kosher salt
¼	cup dry sherry
½	cup low-sodium beef broth
12	oz broccoli florets or trimmed green beans, or a mix
1	cup shredded carrots
1	red bell pepper, cored and cut into thin strips
¼	cup soy sauce
2	Tbsp oyster sauce
2	Tbsp rice vinegar
2	Tbsp orange juice concentrate
1	Tbsp chili garlic sauce, or more to taste
2	tsp cornstarch
1	Tbsp finely chopped peeled fresh ginger
1	Tbsp finely chopped garlic
2	scallions, sliced
	Steamed rice, for serving
	Cilantro sprigs, for garnish

Active time: 15 min.

Pressure time: 1 min.

Total time: 25 min.

Pressure level: Low

Release: Quick

Serves: 4

About 530 cal
23 g fat (11 g sat)
64 g pro
1,215 mg sodium
12 g carb
3 g fiber

1. Press Sauté on multi-cooker and adjust to High and heat 2 Tbsp oil. Season steak with ½ tsp salt and working in batches as needed, add beef in single layer without crowding and cook until browned, 1½ min. per side; transfer to plate.

2. Wearing oven mitts, pour oil out of multi-cooker. Return to High heat, add sherry and simmer, scraping up any browned bits, then simmer until reduced by half.

3. Add beef broth and ¼ cup water to pot. Put broccoli (or green beans), carrots and bell pepper in steamer basket and place steaks on top. Place steamer basket in multi-cooker. Lock lid and cook on Low pressure 1 min.

4. Use quick-release method to release pressure, then carefully remove lid. Remove steamer basket and transfer steaks to plate.

5. In small bowl, whisk broth and water from multi-cooker with soy sauce, oyster sauce, vinegar, orange juice concentrate, chili sauce and cornstarch. Set aside.

6. Press Sauté and adjust to Medium and heat remaining Tbsp oil. Add ginger, garlic and scallions and cook, stirring, 1 min. Stir in reserved broth mixture and simmer until slightly thickened, 3 min.

7. While sauce cooks, slice steaks ⅛-in. thick. Add beef and vegetables to multi-cooker and stir to coat. Cook just long enough for beef to finish cooking and vegetables to warm. Serve over rice and top with cilantro.

TUNA NOODLE CASSEROLE

Every nostalgic bite of this creamy casserole is loaded with protein, perfectly cooked pasta and decadent cheese, and it's ready in only 30 minutes. What more could you ask for?

1	**Tbsp canola oil**
1	**onion, chopped**
1	**large celery stalk, chopped**
6	**oz wide egg noodles**
1	**bay leaf**
1	**12-oz can evaporated milk, divided**
	Kosher salt
1	**large egg**
1	**tsp cornstarch**
2	**5- to 6-oz cans tuna, drained**
1	**cup frozen peas, thawed**
2	**Tbsp sour cream**
1	**Tbsp heavy cream**
1/2	**cup shredded sharp Cheddar cheese**

Active time: 15 min.

Pressure time: 5 min.

Total time: 25 min.

Pressure level: Low

Release: Quick

Serves: 4

About 450 cal
22 g fat (11 g sat)
35 g pro
770 mg sodium
29 g carb
3 g fiber

1. Press Sauté on multi-cooker and adjust to High and heat oil. Add onion and celery and cook, stirring, 1 min.

2. Stir in noodles, bay leaf, half of evaporated milk, 1 tsp salt and 1 cup water. Lock lid and cook on Low pressure 5 min. Use quick-release method to release pressure and carefully remove lid.

3. In bowl, whisk egg, cornstarch and remaining evaporated milk. Press Sauté and adjust to Low. Add milk mixture and cook, until sauce thickens.

4. Gently stir in tuna and peas and cook until heated through, 2 min. Stir in sour cream and heavy cream, then sprinkle with cheese and let stand 2 min.

SHRIMP SCAMPI

There's a reason this dish is a classic: Shrimp tossed in butter, garlic, white wine and lemon never gets old.

2	Tbsp unsalted butter
3	large cloves garlic, finely chopped
¼	cup dry white wine
½	cup low-sodium chicken broth
1	lb large peeled and deveined shrimp
	Kosher salt and pepper
2	Tbsp lemon juice
	Chopped parsley
	Cooked pasta, for serving

Active time: 5 min.

Pressure time: 1 min.

Total time: 20 min.

Pressure level: High

Release: Quick

Serves: 4

About 160 cal
4 g fat (4 g sat)
22 g pro
320 mg sodium
3 g carb
0 g fiber

1. Press Sauté on multi-cooker; adjust to Medium and melt butter. Add garlic and cook, stirring, 1 min. Add wine and simmer 2 min.

2. Add broth and shrimp, season with ¼ tsp salt and pepper, lock lid and cook on High pressure (12.0) 1 min.

3. Use quick-release method to release pressure, then carefully remove lid and transfer shrimp to bowl. Select Sauté and adjust to High and simmer 2 min. Stir in lemon juice and parsley, then toss with shrimp. Serve over pasta, if desired.

KITCHEN TIP *If using frozen shrimp, choose high-quality ones, and add 1 min. to pressure-cooking time.*

STEAMED COD WITH GINGER-GARLIC BROTH & BABY BOK CHOY

This super simple dinner, flavored with soy, rice wine and grated ginger, lets delicate fish shine.

1	cup fish broth or vegetable broth
2	Tbsp unseasoned rice vinegar
2	Tbsp low-sodium soy sauce
2	Tbsp dry sherry or rice wine
1	Tbsp grated fresh ginger
3	large cloves garlic, finely chopped
4	6- to 8-oz cod fillets
	Kosher salt and pepper
8	oz baby bok choy, trimmed and coarsely chopped
2	scallions, thinly sliced
1	Tbsp toasted sesame oil
	Steamed rice, for serving (optional)

Active time: 10 min.

Pressure time: 2 min.

Total time: 20 min.

Pressure level: Low

Release: Quick

Serves: 4

About 320 cal
6 g fat (0.5 g sat)
56 g pro
870 mg sodium
7 g carb
2 g fiber

1. In multi-cooker, combine fish broth, vinegar, soy sauce, sherry, ginger and garlic. Put steamer trivet or basket in pot. Season cod with ¼ tsp each salt and pepper and place in basket.

2. Scatter bok choy over fillets. Lock lid and cook on Low pressure 2 min.

3. Use quick-release method to release pressure, then carefully remove lid. Carefully remove steamer from multi-cooker.

4. Using large slotted spatula, divide fish and bok choy among four shallow bowls. Spoon broth over fish. Top with scallions and drizzle with sesame oil. Serve with steamed rice, if desired.

KITCHEN TIP *If using frozen cod fillets, increase cooking time by 3 min.*

MUSSELS WITH GARLIC & RED PEPPER SAUCE

Zest up ordinary steamed mussels with sliced fennel, roasted red peppers and a sprinkle of spicy pepper flakes.

1	**Tbsp olive oil**
1	**bulb fennel (fronds reserved), thinly sliced**
4	**cloves garlic, finely chopped**
3	**plum tomatoes, chopped**
1	**roasted red pepper, chopped**
3/4	**cup fish broth, clam juice or water**
1/2	**cup dry white wine**
1/8	**tsp red pepper flakes**
3	**lbs mussels, scrubbed and debearded**
2	**Tbsp heavy cream**
3	**Tbsp coarsely chopped fresh parsley**

Active time: 15 min.

Pressure time: 1 min.

Total time: 20 min.

Pressure level: High

Release: Quick

Serves: 4

About 390 cal
14 g fat (4 g sat)
41 g pro
980 mg sodium
17 g carb
1 g fiber

1. Press Sauté on multi-cooker; adjust to Medium and heat oil. Add fennel and cook, stirring, 2 min. Add garlic and cook, stirring, 1 min. Stir in tomatoes, roasted pepper, fish broth, wine and red pepper flakes. Stir to combine.

2. Toss with mussels, lock lid and cook on High pressure (12.0) for 1 min.

3. Use quick-release method to release pressure, then carefully remove lid. Check mussels; if they are not opened, replace lid but don't lock in place. Let mussels steam 1 min. (Discard any that do not open.)

4. Stir in heavy cream and parsley. Serve in bowls with cooking liquid and sprinkle with fennel fronds.

PEEL & EAT SHRIMP

The spicy-sweet remoulade made for dipping makes this
hands-on dinner even more delicious.

FOR SHRIMP

2	lbs frozen shell-on jumbo (16/25) shrimp
2	Tbsp chopped parsley

FOR REMOULADE

¼	cup plain yogurt
¼	cup mayonnaise
2	Tbsp ketchup
2	Tbsp Creole mustard or other grainy mustard
2	tsp prepared horseradish
½	tsp Worcestershire sauce
2	scallions, finely chopped
2	Tbsp fresh parsley leaves, finely chopped

Active time: 10 min.

Pressure time: 1 min.

Total time: 15 min.

Pressure level: Low

Release: Quick

Serves: 4

About 410 cal
11 g fat (2 g sat)
55 g pro
1,125 mg sodium
21 g carb
1 g fiber

1. Fill large bowl halfway with cold water. Add several handfuls
of ice cubes. Set aside.

2. Put steamer basket into multi-cooker and add 1 cup water.
Arrange shrimp in single layer in steamer basket. Lock lid and
press Steam; adjust to Low pressure and cook 1 min.

3. Use quick-release method to release pressure, then carefully
remove lid and steamer basket. Immediately transfer shrimp to
ice bath.

4. In small bowl, whisk yogurt, mayonnaise, ketchup, mustard,
horseradish, Worcestershire sauce, scallions and parsley. Serve
shrimp sprinkled with parsley and remoulade, for dipping.

KITCHEN TIP *Don't use shrimp any smaller than 26/30 per pound; they will overcook in the pressure cooker.*

"BBQ" Salmon & Brussels Bake, recipe on p 113

SIMPLE SHEET PAN DINNERS

3

When it comes to foolproof family dinners, nothing is more forgiving than roasting, baking and broiling. These high-temperature techniques are hassle-free and hands-off. Most important, these methods develop great flavor and can be done on one versatile piece of equipment—a sheet pan.

THE ONLY PAN YOU NEED

A good sheet pan is hard to find. But we've got one—well, 30. We keep that many 18- by 12-in. rimmed baking sheets in the test kitchen. Given their versatility and longevity, sheet pans are a bargain, usually at under $20 apiece. Sometimes labeled "half-sheet pans," they're available at many home supplies stores or online. Use this checklist to make sure you've got a keeper (or two—maybe even 30) in your pantry as well.

- **SIZE.** Pick ones with at least 1-in.-high sides. They allow for great browning but still catch pan juices.
- **ALUMINUM COATING.** We prefer aluminum-coated steel or aluminum to nonstick pans. The surface of aluminum sheet pans ensures that vegetables, meats and sweets brown beautifully. It also doesn't scratch easily, which means it lasts longer.

● **COLOR.** We've learned that dark-colored pans hold too much heat and overbrown foods. So go light—even if you chose a baking sheet with a nonstick finish.

SHEET PAN VS. JELLY-ROLL PAN

A sheet pan is a metal sheet with one or two (or all) sides bent up for easier handling. Its design allows air to circulate freely around the food so it bakes and browns evenly. A jelly-roll pan or rimmed baking sheet (either 15½- by 10½-in. or 18- by 12- in. a.k.a. a half-sheet pan) has 1-in.-high sides and is perfect for making cake rolls; it can stand in for a sheet pan in a pinch. It is also a terrific roasting pan for veggies and more. For the recipes in this section, either a sheet pan or jelly-roll pan will be effective.

VEGETABLE ROASTING 101

You can roast just about anything, but vegetables especially benefit from the high, dry heat of the oven. Their flavor becomes concentrated and their natural sugars caramelize, transforming them into richly satisfying sides.

Refer to this helpful chart for cutting instructions, cooking times and seasoning suggestions for perfect oven-roasted veggies every time. For every 2 lbs of vegetables, toss with 1 Tbsp of olive oil prior to roasting. Spread the vegetables on a sheet pan in a single layer, with space between the vegetables to allow heat to circulate around them. If the vegetables are overcrowded, they will steam rather than brown. Also, you can roast different vegetables together if their cooking times are similar, so mix it up!

VEGETABLE ROASTING GUIDE

VEGETABLES	HOW TO CUT	ROASTING TIME AT 450°F	GREAT GARNISHES
Asparagus	Trim	10 to 15 min.	Sprinkle with lemon zest
Beets (without tops)	Whole, unpeeled, pricked with a fork, then peeled after roasting 1 hr.	1 hr.	Peel, cut in pieces, season with salt, pepper and fresh orange zest

VEGETABLES	HOW TO CUT	ROASTING TIME AT 450°F	GREAT GARNISHES
Broccoli	Trim and peel stem, split florets into 1½-in.-wide pieces	10 to 15 min.	Sprinkle with grated Parmesan or extra-sharp Cheddar
Brussels Sprouts	Trim and halve through stem end	15 to 20 min.	Toss with maple syrup immediately after roasting
Butternut Squash	1-in. pieces	25 to 35 min.	Toss with fresh thyme before roasting
Carrots	Peeled and halved or quartered lengthwise, if thick	20 to 30 min.	Toss with ground cumin and coriander before roasting
Cauliflower	1½-in. florets	20 to 30 min.	Sprinkle with chopped fresh parsley and crushed red pepper flakes
Eggplant	½-in.-thick slices	20 to 25 min.	Drizzle with extra virgin olive oil
Green Beans	Trim	10 to 15 min.	Toss with chopped fresh dill, tarragon or chives
Onions	Cut into wedges	20 to 30 min.	Toss with balsamic vinegar and roast 5 min. more
Potatoes	Cut into 1-in.-thick wedges	25 to 30 min.	Toss with fresh rosemary before roasting
Sweet Peppers	1-in.-wide strips	15 to 25 min.	Toss with chopped parsley, a splash of vinegar and season with salt and pepper
Sweet Potatoes	Cut into 1-in.-thick wedges	25 to 30 min.	Toss with crushed coriander seed before roasting
Turnips	Peel and cut into 6 wedges	20 to 30 min.	Toss with chopped fresh mint
Zucchini	Halve crosswise then quarter each half lengthwise	15 to 20 min.	Toss with grated Parmesan, lemon zest and chopped scallion

SHEET PAN CARE AND MAINTENANCE

DEALING WITH GREASE AND GRIME

Give baked-on food the one-two punch by dialing up your dish soap with a sprinkle of baking soda. "Hot-water soak, mildly abrasive baking soda, a scrub sponge and some elbow grease is all you need to dissolve stuck-on grease," says Carolyn Forte, director of the Cleaning Lab at the Good Housekeeping Institute. Follow these steps to keep your favorite baking sheets in tip-top shape.

1. Coat the bottom of the pan with baking soda and dish soap.

2. Let it soak in hot water for 15 minutes.

3. Use a sponge and continue to sprinkle more baking soda over the stubborn spots as you scrub. The abrasion from the baking soda will easily lift the grime away.

STORING SHEET PANS

It's awful when you have to fish out the biggest pan from the bottom of a pile of stacked lasagna dishes and baking trays. Your aluminum sheets may have a better chance at withstanding the friction between pans and dishes, but your nonstick ones will not last long. Try using a wire rack organizer to keep your sheet pans neat, tidy and easily accessible. Your sheet pans will thank you for it.

SHEET PAN RECIPES

MEDITERRANEAN CHICKEN BAKE

Chicken, potatoes and greens make an all-in-one meal that gets an extra flavor boost from fresh thyme and roasted lemon.

1	lb potatoes, cut into ¾-in. pieces
½	cup green olives
2	tsp fresh thyme leaves
3	Tbsp olive oil, divided
	Kosher salt and pepper
1	lemon, halved
1	tsp paprika
4	small chicken legs, split (4 drumsticks and 4 thighs; about 2½ lbs)
4	cups baby kale

Active time: 10 min.

Total time: 40 min.

Serves: 4

About 470 cal
26 g fat (5.5 g sat)
38 g pro
775 mg sodium
1 g carb
4 g fiber

1. Heat oven to 425°F. On large rimmed baking sheet, toss potatoes, olives and thyme with 2 Tbsp oil and ¼ tsp each salt and pepper. Place lemon halves, cut-sides down, on baking sheet.

2. In bowl, combine paprika, remaining Tbsp oil and ½ tsp each salt and pepper. Rub mixture all over chicken and transfer to baking sheet, nestling it among vegetables.

3. Roast chicken and vegetables until chicken is golden brown and cooked through (165°F), 25 to 30 min.

4. Transfer chicken to plates, scatter kale evenly over vegetables remaining in pan and return to oven until kale is just beginning to wilt, about 1 min. Fold kale into potatoes, squeeze juice of lemons over vegetables and serve with chicken.

HERBED RICOTTA & FRESH TOMATO TART

Store-bought puff pastry and a one-pan method gets this show-stopping dinner done pronto.

1	sheet frozen puff pastry (from 17.3-oz pkg.), thawed
1	large egg, beaten
1	cup ricotta cheese
	Kosher salt and pepper
1	lemon
2	scallions, finely chopped
1/2	cup fresh flat-leaf parsley, chopped
1	lb heirloom tomatoes (various colors and sizes), sliced or halved
2	Tbsp olive oil
1/4	cup small fresh mint leaves
	Flaky sea salt, for sprinkling

Active time: 15 min.

Total time: 40 min.

Serves: 6

About 300 cal
21 g fat (9.5 g sat)
0 g pro
280 mg sodium
25 g carb
2 g fiber

1. Heat oven to 425°F and place oven rack in lower third of oven. Unfold pastry onto piece of parchment paper and roll 1/2 in. bigger on all sides. Slide parchment (and pastry) onto baking sheet.

2. Using paring knife, score 1/2-in. border all the way around pastry. Lightly brush border with egg. Using fork, poke middle of pastry all over, then bake until golden brown, 20 to 25 min.

3. Meanwhile, in medium bowl, combine ricotta and 1/4 tsp each salt and pepper. Finely grate zest of lemon into bowl and squeeze in 2 tsp juice; mix to combine. Fold in scallions and parsley. Spread onto middle of pastry.

4. Arrange tomatoes on tart, drizzle with oil and sprinkle with mint, sea salt and freshly ground pepper.

STEAK WITH BEANS & BROCCOLINI

Roasting steaks is our favorite splatter-free technique.

1	**lb small cremini mushrooms, trimmed and halved**
1	**bunch Broccolini, trimmed and cut into 2-in. lengths**
4	**cloves garlic, finely chopped**
2	**Tbsp olive oil**
¼-½	**tsp red pepper flakes**
	Kosher salt and pepper
2	**1-in.-thick New York strip steaks (about 1½ lbs total), trimmed of excess fat**
1	**15-oz can low-sodium cannellini beans, rinsed**

Active time: 20 min.

Total time: 50 min.

Serves: 4

About 400 cal
13 g fat (3 g sat fat)
48 g pro
550 mg sodium
23 g carb
5 g fiber

1. Heat oven to 450°F. On large rimmed baking sheet, toss mushrooms, Broccolini, garlic, oil, red pepper flakes and ¼ tsp each salt and pepper. Roast 15 min.

2. Push mixture to edges of pan to make room for steaks. Season steaks with ¼ tsp each salt and pepper and place in center of pan. Roast steaks to desired doneness, 5 to 7 min. per side for medium-rare. Transfer steaks to cutting board and let rest 5 min. before slicing.

3. Add beans to baking sheet and toss to combine. Roast until heated through, about 3 min. Serve beans and vegetables with steak.

FISH CHOWDER SHEET PAN BAKE

All the flavors of your favorite chowder, but the crispy panko topping with mustard and lemon zest provides a satisfying crunch to the tender, flaky fish.

1	lb small yellow potatoes (about 16), halved lengthwise
2	small red onions, cut into ½-in.-thick wedges
4	slices bacon, cut into ½-in. pieces
1	Tbsp mayonnaise
1	Tbsp Dijon mustard
1	tsp finely grated lemon zest
¼	cup panko
1	Tbsp olive oil
1	Tbsp thyme leaves
4	6-oz pieces cod fillet (at least 1 in. thick)
	Black pepper

Active time: 15 min.

Total time: 30 min.

Serves: 4

About 410 cal
18 g fat (5 g sat)
33 g pro
435 mg sodium
28 g carb
3 g fiber

1. Heat oven to 450°F. Pile potatoes and onions in center of rimmed baking sheet and place bacon on top. Roast 10 min.

2. Meanwhile, in small bowl, combine mayonnaise, mustard and lemon zest. In second small bowl, combine panko with oil, then fold in thyme. Season fish with ½ tsp pepper, then spread with mayonnaise mixture and sprinkle with panko.

3. Remove baking sheet from oven and reduce oven temperature to 425°F. Toss potatoes and onion mixture together, then spread in an even layer, arranging potatoes cut-side down.

4. Nestle fish pieces among vegetables and roast until fish is opaque throughout and potatoes are golden brown and tender, 12 to 15 min.

SWEET POTATO & CHORIZO PIZZA

Roasted sweet potatoes paired with spicy chorizo makes an unlikely topper that you wouldn't find with delivery pizza.

Cornmeal, for dusting

1 lb pizza dough (thawed if frozen), left out at room temperature for 30 min.

1 medium sweet potato (about 8 oz), peeled and thinly sliced

1 small red onion, thinly sliced

1 Tbsp olive oil

1 tsp finely chopped fresh rosemary

Kosher salt and pepper

3 oz Spanish chorizo, thinly sliced

1/3 lb thinly sliced provolone (from the deli counter, 6 to 7 slices)

Green salad, for serving

Active time: 15 min.

Total time: 30 min.

Serves: 4

About 560 cal
24.5 g fat (10 g sat)
22 g pro
1,600 mg sodium
59 g carb
4 g fiber

1. Heat oven to 475°F. Dust baking sheet with cornmeal or line with parchment paper. Shape dough into 16-in. circle, oval or rectangle and place on prepared baking sheet.

2. In large bowl, toss potato, onion, oil, rosemary, 1/4 tsp salt and 1/2 tsp pepper. Add chorizo and cheese and toss to combine.

3. Scatter vegetable-chorizo mixture over dough and bake until potatoes are tender and crust is golden brown and crisp, about 15 min. Serve with a salad, if desired.

ROASTED SHRIMP SCAMPI

Skip the spaghetti and try tender, twirl-able zucchini "noodles" for a
light dinner that comes together on one pan.

1½	lbs spiralized zucchini
2	Tbsp olive oil, divided
	Kosher salt and pepper
20	large peeled and deveined shrimp
4	scallions, thinly sliced
4	cloves garlic, thinly sliced
1	small red chile, thinly sliced
2	Tbsp dry white wine
1	Tbsp fresh lemon juice
4	oz feta cheese, crumbled

Active time: 10 min.

Total time: 25 min.

Serves: 4

About 200 cal
13.5 g fat (5.5 g sat)
11 g pro
715 mg sodium
10 g carb
2 g fiber

1. Heat oven to 475°F. On large rimmed baking sheet, toss
zucchini with 1 Tbsp oil and ¼ tsp each salt and pepper;
arrange in even layer and roast 6 min.

2. Meanwhile, in bowl, toss shrimp, scallions, garlic and chile
with wine, lemon juice and ¼ tsp each salt and pepper.

3. Scatter shrimp over zucchini, drizzle with remaining Tbsp oil
and sprinkle with feta. Roast until shrimp is opaque throughout,
5 to 7 min.

MEDITERRANEAN PITA PIZZAS

Topped with spiced ground beef, peppery arugula, creamy yogurt sauce and crunchy almonds, these tasty personal pitas make weeknight cooking so much more fun.

8	oz lean ground beef (at least 90% lean)
1	small red onion (about 4 oz), half finely chopped and half thinly sliced
1	clove garlic, finely chopped
1	tsp hot sauce
1	tsp ground cumin
1/2	tsp ground coriander
1/2	tsp grated lemon zest, plus 2 Tbsp lemon juice
	Kosher salt and pepper
4	pita breads
1	tsp olive oil
4	cups baby arugula
1/4	cup plain yogurt
2	Tbsp sliced almonds, toasted and roughly chopped

Active time: 25 min.

Total time: 25 min.

Serves: 4

About 325 cal
9.5. g fat (3 g sat)
19 g pro
680 mg sodium
40 g carb
3 g fiber

1. Heat oven to 400°F. In a large bowl, combine beef, chopped onion, garlic, hot sauce, cumin, coriander, lemon zest, and 1/2 tsp each salt and pepper; set aside.

2. Arrange pitas on rimmed baking sheet and bake 3 min., then remove from oven and flip over.

3. Divide beef mixture among pitas, spreading to edges. Bake until sizzling and pitas are golden brown and crisp around edges, 10 to 12 min.

4. Meanwhile, toss sliced onion with oil, 1 Tbsp lemon juice and pinch each salt and pepper. Before serving, fold in arugula. Divide among pitas, then drizzle with yogurt mixed with remaining Tbsp lemon juice and sprinkle with almonds.

KITCHEN TIP *Cooking the ground beef directly on top of the pita gives you maximum flavor with minimal effort, since the oils from the meat help crisp up the bread. Use at least 90% lean beef so the excess fat doesn't make it soggy instead.*

ALMOND-CRUSTED CREOLE SALMON

Don't have almonds in the pantry? Use finely chopped
pistachios or pecans as a substitution.

1	**lb green beans, trimmed**
1	**Tbsp olive oil**
	Kosher salt and pepper
4	**6-oz skinless salmon fillets**
1/3	**cup nonfat Greek yogurt**
2	**tsp Creole seasoning**
1	**tsp finely grated lemon zest**
2	**cups almonds, coarsely chopped**

Active time: 10 min.

Total time: 25 min.

Serves: 4

About 310 cal
13g fat (2 g sat)
39 g pro
540 mg sodium
9 g carb
4 g fiber

1. Heat oven to 450°F. On large rimmed baking sheet, toss
green beans with oil and ¼ tsp each salt and pepper. Push
to one side of pan.

2. Place salmon on other side of pan. In small bowl, combine
yogurt, Creole seasoning and lemon zest. Spread yogurt
mixture on salmon fillets and then top each fillet with almonds.

3. Lightly spray salmon with olive oil cooking spray. Roast
until salmon is opaque throughout and green beans are tender,
12 to 15 min.

KITCHEN TIP *Trimming green beans can be done in a snap. Use a
chef's knife to cut off the knobby ends with one slice by lining up the
stems to face the same direction.*

"BBQ" SALMON & BRUSSELS BAKE

The sugar in this savory rub caramelizes as the salmon roasts.
And leftovers can be tossed with a salad for lunch!

3/4	**lb Brussels sprouts, trimmed and halved**
2	**Tbsp olive oil, divided**
	Kosher salt and pepper
1	**Tbsp brown sugar**
1/2	**tsp garlic powder**
1/2	**tsp onion powder**
1/2	**tsp smoked paprika**
4	**6-oz pieces skinless salmon fillet**
	Chopped chives, for serving

Active time: 15 min.

Total time: 30 min.

Serves: 4

About 280 cal
11 g fat (2 g sat)
35 g pro
380 mg sodium
11 g carb
3 g fiber

1. Heat oven to 450°F. On large rimmed baking sheet, toss Brussels sprouts with 1 Tbsp oil and ¼ tsp each salt and pepper; roast 8 min.

2. Meanwhile, in small bowl, stir together brown sugar, garlic powder, onion powder, smoked paprika, ½ tsp salt and remaining Tbsp oil.

3. Brush rub all over salmon, nestle salmon among sprouts and roast until salmon is opaque throughout and sprouts are golden brown and tender, 12 to 15 min. more. Serve sprinkled with chives, if desired.

KITCHEN TIP *The size of a Brussels sprout indicates its flavor—the smaller the sprout the more tender and sweet. Larger sprouts will taste like cabbage.*

SHEET PAN ITALIAN SAUSAGE & PEPPER BAKE

This fair-goer favorite gets lightened up with turkey sausage and tons of garlic and oregano-spiced vegetables.

2	peppers (orange, red or a combination), halved, seeded and thickly sliced
1	pint cherry or grape tomatoes, halved
1	medium yellow onion, cut into 1-in. wedges
1	clove garlic, finely chopped
1	Tbsp olive oil
1	tsp dried oregano
	Kosher salt and pepper
4	sweet or hot Italian turkey sausages (about 12 oz), cut into 1½-in. pieces

Active time: 10 min.

Total time: 30 min.

Serves: 4

About 210 cal
13 g fat (0.5 g sat)
16 g pro
665 mg sodium
10 g carb
2 g fiber

1. Heat oven to 400°F. On large rimmed baking sheet, toss peppers, tomatoes, onion and garlic with oil, oregano, ¼ tsp salt and ½ tsp pepper, then toss with sausages.

2. Roast until sausages are cooked through and beginning to blister and vegetables are golden brown and tender, 15 to 20 min.

BAKED HALIBUT WITH POTATOES & BRUSSELS SPROUTS

The fresh herb dressing does double duty here: It gets tossed with the vegetables at the beginning and slathered on the fish at the end.

2	**Tbsp olive oil**
2	**Tbsp chopped mixed fresh herbs (such as parsley, thyme and rosemary)**
	Kosher salt and pepper
1	**lb fingerling potatoes (about 20), halved lengthwise**
1	**lb Brussels sprouts (about 10), trimmed and quartered**
1	**large shallot, cut into wedges**
1½	**lbs halibut fillet**

Active time: 20 min.

Total time: 30 min.

Serves: 4

About 370 cal
9 g fat (2 g sat)
40 g pro
505 mg sodium
37 g carb
7 g fiber

1. Heat oven to 425°F. In bowl, whisk together oil, herbs, ¾ tsp salt and ½ tsp pepper.

2. On large rimmed baking sheet, toss potatoes, Brussels sprouts and shallot with half of oil mixture. Arrange potatoes cut-side down; roast 10 min.

3. Remove pan from oven and set fish atop vegetables. Brush fish with remaining oil mixture and roast until potatoes are golden brown and tender and fish is opaque throughout, about 15 min. more.

KITCHEN TIP *Pureed cottage cheese is a great replacement for ricotta, thanks to its similar texture, but with fewer calories and less fat.*

SPINACH & ARTICHOKE PIZZA

Your favorite dip combined with your favorite food (pizza, of course!) makes this dinner the ultimate better-for-you comfort food.

Flour, for surface

1 lb pizza dough (thawed if frozen), left at room temperature for 30 min.

Cornmeal, for baking sheet

3 cups baby spinach

1 14-oz can artichoke hearts, drained, patted very dry, and chopped

2 cloves garlic, thinly sliced

1 Tbsp olive oil

Kosher salt and pepper

½ cup small-curd 1% cottage cheese

2 Tbsp grated Pecorino Romano cheese

2 tsp finely grated lemon zest

½ oz Parmesan cheese

Active time: 10 min.

Total time: 25 min.

Serves: 4

About 385 cal
8 g fat (2 g sat)
19 g pro
1,110 mg sodium
60 g carb
3 g fiber

1. Heat oven to 500°F (if you can't heat oven this high without broiling, heat it to 475°F).

2. On lightly floured surface, shape dough into 14-in. oval. Place on cornmeal-dusted baking sheet.

3. In a bowl, toss spinach, artichoke hearts, garlic, oil and ¼ tsp pepper.

4. In mini food processor, puree cottage cheese, Pecorino, lemon zest and ¼ tsp each salt and pepper.

5. Scatter spinach-artichoke mixture onto dough first, then dollop with cheese mixture, grate Parmesan on top and bake until crust is golden brown, 10 to 12 min.

ROASTED SALMON WITH GREEN BEANS & TOMATOES

Perfectly roasted salmon doesn't need much, but garlic, olives and anchovy provide even better flavor.

6	cloves garlic, smashed
1¼	lbs green beans, trimmed
1	pint grape tomatoes
½	cup pitted kalamata olives
3	anchovy fillets, chopped (optional)
2	Tbsp olive oil, divided
	Kosher salt and pepper
1¼	lbs skinless salmon fillet, cut into 4 pieces
	Greek yogurt, for serving

Active time: 15 min.

Total time: 20 min.

Serves: 4

About 330 cal
15 g fat (3 g sat)
31 g pro
445 mg sodium
15 g carb
5 g fiber

1. Heat oven to 425°F. On large rimmed baking sheet, toss garlic, beans, tomatoes, olives and anchovies (if using) with 1 Tbsp oil and ¼ tsp pepper. Roast until vegetables are tender and beginning to brown, 12 to 15 min.

2. Meanwhile, heat remaining Tbsp oil in large skillet on medium. Season salmon with ¼ tsp each salt and pepper and cook until golden brown and opaque throughout, 4 to 5 min. per side. Serve with vegetables and yogurt, if desired.

ASIAN TOFU WITH BABY BOK CHOY

Tofu glazed in a spicy-sweet sauce makes going meatless easier—and more delicious—than ever.

1	**14-oz pkg. extra-firm tofu**
4	**tsp low-sodium soy sauce**
1	**Tbsp chili garlic sauce**
1	**clove garlic, pressed**
1	**tsp honey**
6	**tsp toasted sesame oil, divided**
	Vegetable oil, for baking sheet
8	**small heads baby bok choy, trimmed and halved**
4	**sugar snap peas, thinly sliced**
½	**tsp black sesame seeds**

Active time: 20 min.

Total time: 30 min.

Serves: 4

About 195 cal
12.5 g fat (1.5 g sat)
13 g pro
380 mg sodium
10 g carb
4 g fiber

1. Place tofu on rimmed baking sheet between paper towels. Top with another baking sheet and weigh down with heavy cans or skillet; let sit at least 5 min. (If you have the time, let sit for up to 30 min.)

2. Meanwhile, combine soy sauce, chili garlic sauce, garlic, honey and 4 tsp sesame oil.

3. Heat oven to 400°F. Transfer tofu to cutting board. Wipe off baking sheet and lightly oil. Slice tofu into ½-in.-thick triangles and arrange on prepared sheet. Drizzle with 1 Tbsp sauce mixture and bake until top is golden, 12 to 15 min.

4. Turn tofu over, arrange on one side of baking sheet and drizzle with 1 Tbsp sauce mixture. Arrange bok choy on other half of sheet and gently toss with remaining 2 tsp sesame oil.

5. Roast until tofu is golden brown and bok choy is tender, 10 min. more. Drizzle remaining sauce over tofu and sprinkle everything with snap peas and sesame seeds.

FENNEL ROASTED CHICKEN & PEPPERS

Toasted fennel seeds and orange zest season both the chicken and the vegetables for maximum flavor. Creamy bits of feta sprinkled on top provide the perfect salty bite.

1	Tbsp fennel seeds
1	Tbsp finely grated orange zest
3	bell peppers (red, yellow and orange), cut into 1-in. chunks
3	cloves garlic, thinly sliced
3	Tbsp olive oil, divided
	Kosher salt and pepper
4	small chicken legs (about 2 lbs)
4	cups baby spinach
2	oz feta cheese, crumbled

Active time: 15 min.

Total time: 30 min.

Serves: 4

About 530 cal
40 g fat (11 g sat)
32 g pro
495 mg sodium
11 g carb
3 g fiber

1. Heat oven to 425°F. In small skillet, toast fennel seeds and orange zest until lightly browned and fragrant, 3 to 4 min. Transfer to spice grinder or blender and pulse to blend and grind. Set aside.

2. On large rimmed baking sheet, toss bell peppers and garlic with 2 Tbsp oil and ½ tsp each salt and pepper.

3. Rub chicken legs with remaining Tbsp oil, then with fennel-orange mixture. Nestle among vegetables on one baking sheet and roast both sheets until chicken is golden brown and cooked through and peppers are tender, 20 to 25 min.

4. Transfer chicken to plates, scatter spinach over peppers remaining on sheet and toss until just beginning to wilt. Sprinkle with feta and serve with chicken.

ROASTED CAULIFLOWER PIZZA

Sweet-tender roasted cauliflower and onions sink in to melty Gruyère cheese for the most mouthwatering vegetarian dinner.

Flour, for surface

1 lb pizza dough (thawed if frozen), left at room temperature for 30 min.

Cornmeal, for baking sheet

½ medium head (about 1 lb) cauliflower, thinly sliced

1 small red onion, thinly sliced

½ cup fresh flat-leaf parsley

2 Tbsp olive oil

¼ tsp crushed red pepper (optional)

Kosher salt

4 oz Gruyère cheese, coarsely grated (about 1¾ cups)

Active time: 10 min.

Total time: 30 min.

Serves: 4

About 335 cal
16 g fat (6 g sat)
15 g pro
740 mg sodium
32 g carb
1.5 g fiber

1. Heat oven to 500°F (if you can't heat oven this high without broiling, heat it to 475°F).

2. On lightly floured surface, shape dough into 14-in. oval. Place on cornmeal-dusted baking sheet.

3. In large bowl, toss cauliflower, onion, parsley, oil, crushed red pepper (if using) and ½ tsp salt; fold in Gruyère.

4. Scatter vegetables over dough and bake until cauliflower is tender and crust is golden brown, 12 to 15 min.

OVEN-ROASTED SALMON WITH CHARRED LEMON VINAIGRETTE

Fresh lemon juice whisked together with stone-ground mustard and olive oil creates a snappy dressing for roasted salmon and vegetables.

1	lemon
2	bulbs fennel, thinly sliced
2	small red onions, thinly sliced
2½	Tbsp olive oil, divided
	Kosher salt and pepper
1¼	lbs skin-on salmon fillet
1	tsp stone-ground mustard
3	cups baby arugula

Active time: 15 min.

Total time: 30 min.

Serves: 4

About 305 cal
14 g fat (2.5 g sat)
31 g pro
400 mg sodium
14 g carb
5 g fiber

1. Heat broiler. Cut pointed ends off lemon, halve crosswise, and place on rimmed baking sheet, center-cut-sides up. Broil on top rack until charred, 5 min.; transfer to plate and set aside.

2. Reduce oven temperature to 425°F. On same baking sheet, toss fennel and onions with 1½ Tbsp oil and ¼ tsp each salt and pepper; arrange around edges of sheet. Place salmon in center of sheet and season with ¼ tsp each salt and pepper. Roast until vegetables are tender and salmon is opaque throughout, 17 to 20 min.

3. Juice charred lemon halves into small bowl and whisk in mustard and remaining Tbsp oil. Remove baking sheet from oven and fold arugula into vegetables. Drizzle charred lemon vinaigrette over fish and vegetables and gently toss vegetables.

KITCHEN TIP *Charring citrus fruits like lemons helps loosen up and release juices while also adding a slight smoky flavor. This method works well on the grill too.*

BALSAMIC-ROSEMARY PORK

Roasted grapes provide the perfect juicy burst of sweetness to pair
with savory pork and caramelized fennel.

2³/₄	lbs pork tenderloins
3	Tbsp balsamic vinegar, divided
2	Tbsp olive oil, divided
1	Tbsp chopped fresh rosemary plus 1 sprig, halved
	Kosher salt and pepper
2	small bulbs fennel, cut into ½-in.-thick wedges
2	small shallots, sliced
12	oz small red seedless grapes (about 2½ cups)

Active time: 15 min.

Total time: 30 min.

Serves: 4

About 370 cal
13 g fat (3 g sat)
37 g pro
500 mg sodium
26 g carb
4 g fiber

1. Heat oven to 475°F. Working on rimmed baking sheet,
coat pork with 2 Tbsp vinegar, then 1 Tbsp oil. Season with
chopped fresh rosemary and ½ tsp each salt and pepper;
roast 8 min.

2. Meanwhile, toss fennel and shallots with remaining Tbsp
oil, rosemary sprig, and ¼ tsp each salt and pepper. Scatter
around pork and roast until pork reaches 135°F on an
instant-read thermometer, 8 to 10 min.

3. Transfer pork to cutting board and let rest at least 5 min.
before slicing. Toss grapes and remaining Tbsp vinegar with
vegetables on pan and continue roasting until fennel is golden
brown and tender and grapes begin to burst, about 8 min.
Serve with pork and any pan juices.

Charred Shrimp, Leek & Asparagus Skewers, recipe on p 144

4

NO-SWEAT GRILLING

Grilling must be one of our favorite ways to cook food. It's fast, easy to clean up and doesn't take much effort to whip up crazy-flavorful foods. It may seem intimidating to the novice home cook, but we're here to get you all fired up.

GRILL BUYER'S GUIDE

● **TYPE.** There are an assortment of grills to choose from, including gas, charcoal, electric, and pellet. Each have their pros and cons, which you can read about below.

● **SIZE.** Consider how many people you will be cooking for, and how often. Size affects price, amount of needed fuel, and storing ability.

● **PORTABILITY.** Most grills are equipped with wheels, folding shelves, and a secure fuel holder, which make it easier to face away from the wind or move for storage.

● **SIDE TABLES.** Large, sturdy surface areas are your friend when it comes to prepping and serving; use them for organizing and a more smooth-running assembly line.

● **SIDE BURNER.** An additional cooking option offers versatility for heating sides or warming sauces; look for options with a cover that can double as surface area when not in use.

✓ **ACCESSORIES.** Some grills offer unique features like rotisserie spits, pizza stones, and multiple fuel options that are worth considering if you want to take your grill to the next level.

WHAT TYPE OF GRILL IS BEST?

When considering a new outdoor grill, the two biggest players are gas and charcoal, but electric and wood pellet grills are also fair game. When selecting what type of grill to buy, consider how often you'll be grilling, the amount of space you have for storage, what flavor you prefer and the amount of time and attention you'll want to spend cooking. Here are the basics on each:

GAS GRILLS are the most common type. Gas grills are great because they offer excellent control over cooking temp (the ability to adjust the burner knobs makes it less likely that you'll end up with burnt food), plus they ignite with the push of a button, heat up quickly and are easy to clean. It's the go-to option for no-fuss grillers who plan to barbecue frequently. Just keep in mind that you'll need fuel from a propane tank or natural gas line on your property.

CHARCOAL GRILLS require briquettes or lump charcoal to ignite. Charcoal is more hands-on and takes time to heat up and cool down but imparts a better, more barbecue-y flavor than gas because it often gets hotter. For grilling purists willing to work for it.

ELECTRIC GRILLS plug in and can't be beat for ease-of-use or convenience—especially the grills that can be used indoors or at apartment complexes that don't allow grills—just don't expect steaks or burgers "browned" on an electric grill to taste like the ones from a real BBQ.

PELLET GRILLS are a growing category that use hardwood pellets made out of wood scraps to heat. Pellets provide a delicious, authentic hardwood flavor to food but are costly and may be hard to track down.

HOW TO MAINTAIN YOUR GRILL

AT THE START AND END OF GRILLING SEASON

These speedy tips from the Good Housekeeping Institute Cleaning Lab come from years of testing outdoor grills, as well as the cleaners and tools you need to keep them working well (and your food tasting great).

The Three Main Steps

1. Remove and clean the grates
2. Clean the grill's interior
3. Clean the grill's exterior

STEP 1: How to Clean BBQ Grill Grates

These are the workhorses of your cooker and because they come in direct contact with your food, they need to be clean. Start by removing the cool grates and wiping or brushing off as much of the big, loose debris as you can with a mesh or nylon scrub pad or a brush. In a sink or large bucket, mix up a sudsy solution of a grease-cutting dish liquid, like Dawn, and hot water and place the grates in to soak. If they don't completely fit in, immerse one half, soak, then flip it over to get the other side. After soaking 15 to 30 min., put on some rubber gloves and scrub the grates clean with a sturdy grill brush or scrubbing pad. Take extra care with porcelain grates, because you don't want to damage them.

STEP 2: How to Clean the Inside of a BBQ Grill

With the grates removed, brush down the inside to clear out any loose particles that have collected in the bottom and around the sides. Scrape off any large peeling flakes of carbon and grease, and if yours is a charcoal grill, empty the ash catcher. Don't forget to clean the drip pan and grease cup in warm soapy water and line them with aluminum foil so they'll be easier to clean next time.

STEP 3: How to Clean the Exterior of a BBQ Grill

Mix another batch of warm sudsy dish liquid and water and wipe down the exterior, handle, side trays and any bottom doors with a sponge or cloth or use a grease-cutting all-purpose cleaner. Rinse and buff dry. For stainless steel surfaces, use a cleaner made for stainless steel appliances to banish streaks.

BEFORE OR AFTER EVERY USE

We like to keep a brush close by—made of steel or another material that won't melt—to clean grill grates when they are still hot. Grates can also be scrubbed down before lighting the grill, which allows any loosened residue to burn off while it preheats. Remember to check your brushes: If any of the bristles are loose, it's time to change the head or get a new brush (loose bristles could accidentally come off and get lodged in food).

GRILLING CHEAT SHEET

You can toss just about anything on the grill. Here, some quick tips for our favorite open-flame fare.

FOOD	HEAT	TIME	TIPS
Burgers	Direct (uncovered), medium-high	4 to 5 min. per side for medium	To help the patty stay flat, use your thumb to make a shallow 1½-in.-wide indent in the top of each patty. Grill them indent-side up first.
Hot Dogs	Direct (uncovered), medium-high	6 to 8 min., turning occasionally	To prevent dogs from falling through the grill grates, line them up perpendicular to the grates. Then, use a long spatula to roll them all rather than turning each one individually.
Turkey Burgers	Direct (uncovered), medium-high	4 to 7 min. per side	Avoid the urge to press down on the patties while they cook, or you will squeeze out some of the tasty juices and make the burger dry.
Skirt Steak (½ to ¾ in. thick)	Direct (uncovered), medium-high	3 to 5 min. per side for medium-rare	Cut it crosswise into 4- to 5-in. pieces, for easier flipping. Always cut against the grain, meaning you should avoid cutting on the short end of the steak.
Flank Steak (¾ to 1 in. thick)	Direct (uncovered), medium-high	4 to 6 min. per side for medium-rare	Try rubbing meat with spices (omit the salt for now!) or toss it with a mixture of soy sauce, grated garlic and ginger. Refrigerate for up to 8 hr. before grilling for maximum flavor.

FOOD	HEAT	TIME	TIPS
London Broil/ Sirloin	Direct (uncovered), medium-high	5 to 7 min. per side for medium-rare	You can grill this steak whole and then slice it. Or cut the steak into smaller pieces before grilling to give each person their own steak.
Sausage	Direct (covered), medium-high	10 to 14 min., turning occasionally	Try brushing balsamic vinegar during the last 5 min. of cooking.
Pork Tenderloin (about 1¼ lbs)	Direct (covered), medium-high	15 to 18 min., turning occasionally (145°F internal temp)	It's best to baste during the last 3 to 6 min. of grilling.
Baby Back Ribs	Indirect (covered), medium-high, then direct (uncovered)	Indirect for 30 to 35 min., followed by direct (uncovered) for 4 to 6 min. per side	If you're going to baste with your favorite sticky sauce, brush and turn every 2 to 3 min. During the last 3 to 6 min. of grilling.
Boneless, Skinless Chicken Breasts	Direct (uncovered), medium	5 to 8 min. per side (165°F internal temp)	If the chicken is getting too charred on the outside, but isn't quite done on the inside, lower the heat and grill covered.
Chicken Wings	Direct (covered), medium-low, turning occasionally	15 to 20 min.	Baste during the last 5 to 6 min. of grilling.
Chicken Drumsticks	Direct (covered), medium-low, turning occasionally	20 to 30 min.	Baste during the last 5 to 6 min. of grilling.
Mussels	Direct (covered), medium-high	About 5 min., until mussels open	Before grilling, scrub shells in cold water, pulling off threads on the side (called the beard).
Lobster	Direct (covered), medium-high, then direct (uncovered)	Grill claws covered for 6 min. Flip claws and add bodies, cut-side down; grill until meat is opaque throughout and shell is bright red, 2 to 3 min. per side	Before putting them on the grill, remove the claws and split the body in half lengthwise.
Squid	Direct (uncovered), medium-high	Grill both tentacles and bodies (place cut-side up first) until opaque throughout, 1 to 2 min. per side	Before putting them on the grill, remove tentacles, then score the tubes crosswise every ¼ in., being careful not to cut all the way through.

FOOD	HEAT	TIME	TIPS
Shrimp	Direct (uncovered), medium-high	Grill until opaque throughout and uniformly pink, 2 to 3 min. per side	Use large, already peeled and deveined ones that won't fall through the grates.
Asparagus	Direct (uncovered), medium-high	4 to 6 min., turning occasionally	Grill asparagus lined up perpendicular to the grill grates, then use a long spatula and roll to rotate, instead of turning each one individually or in groups.
Plum Tomatoes	Direct (uncovered), medium-high	2 to 3 min. per side	Halve tomatoes lengthwise, and start grilling with the cut-side down first.
Zucchini and Summer Squash	Direct (uncovered), medium-high	2 to 5 min. per side	Serve zucchini as is or cut grilled squash into pieces and toss with other ingredients for an easy side.
Eggplant	Direct (uncovered), medium-high	3 to 4 min. per side	Slice small eggplants (about 8 to 12 oz each) into rounds or lengths a bit more than 1/4 in. thick. Brush both sides with olive oil and season with salt and pepper.
Peppers	Direct (uncovered), medium-high	3 to 4 min. per side	Quarter peppers lengthwise and discard seeds. Toss with olive oil, salt and pepper.
Corn	Direct (uncovered), medium-high	3 to 5 min., turning occasionally, until charred	Shuck the corn and rub with olive oil.
Sweet Potatoes	Direct (uncovered), medium-high	10 to 14 min., turning often until tender	Cut sweet potatoes into 1-in.-thick wedges or slice into 1/4-in. rounds.
Peaches and Nectarines	Direct (uncovered), medium-high	1 to 3 min. until charred, cut-side down	Halve or quarter and remove pits prior to throwing them on the grill.
Pineapple	Direct (uncovered), medium-high	2 to 3 min. per side	Remove rind and cut into 1/4-in.-thick triangles or rounds.
Lemon, Lime, Oranges	Direct (uncovered), medium-high	1 to 3 min., cut-side down until charred	Halve or cut into wedges.
Avocado	Direct (uncovered), medium-high	1 to 3 min., cut-side down until charred	Halve and remove pit, leave skin on. Brush lightly with olive oil, then throw on the grill.

GRILLING RECIPES

GRILLED BASIL CHICKEN & ZUCCHINI

The humble chicken tender gets the special treatment in this healthy, basil-infused dish.

1	cup long grain white rice
1	lime, plus wedges for serving
2	cloves garlic
1	Tbsp low-sodium soy sauce
½	tsp sugar
½	red chile, thinly sliced
4	small zucchini (about 1¼ lbs), halved lengthwise
2	Tbsp olive oil, divided
	Kosher salt and pepper
1	lb chicken breast tenders
2½	cups basil, roughly chopped

Active time: 10 min.

Total time: 20 min.

Serves: 4

About 400 cal
10.5 g fat (1.5 g sat)
29 g pro
450 mg sodium
46 g carb
3 g fiber

1. Heat grill to medium-high. Cook rice per pkg. directions.

2. Zest lime into large bowl, then squeeze in 2 Tbsp juice. Finely grate garlic into bowl, then stir in soy sauce, sugar and chile.

3. Brush zucchini with 1 Tbsp oil and season with ¼ tsp each salt and pepper. Rub chicken tenders with remaining Tbsp oil and season with ¼ tsp each salt and pepper. Grill zucchini until just barely tender and chicken until just cooked through, about 3 min. per side; transfer to cutting board.

4. Cut zucchini and chicken into pieces and toss in sauce; fold in basil and serve over rice with lime wedges.

KITCHEN TIP *Subbing in Japanese eggplant for the chicken not only makes this vegetarian but also doubles the fiber and cuts the fat by 2 grams.*

GRILLED STEAK TORTILLA SALAD

Chili-spiced steak, fresh veggies, lime and cilantro tucked into charred tortillas is the fastest way to embrace flavor—and fun!—at dinnertime.

1½	lbs skirt steak, cut crosswise into 4 pieces
1	tsp chili powder
	Kosher salt and pepper
1½	lbs plum tomatoes, cut into pieces
2	scallions, sliced
1	jalapeño, thinly sliced
2	Tbsp fresh lime juice
1	cup fresh cilantro
1	bunch arugula, thick stems discarded
	Charred flour tortillas, for serving

Active time: 10 min.

Total time: 20 min.

Serves: 4

About 340 cal
16.5 g fat (5.5 g sat)
41 g pro
595 mg sodium
9 g carb
3 g fiber

1. Heat grill to medium-high. Season steak with chili powder and ½ tsp each salt and pepper. Grill to desired doneness, 3 to 4 min. per side for medium-rare. Transfer to cutting board and let rest at least 5 min. before slicing.

2. In bowl, toss tomatoes, scallions, jalapeño, lime juice, ½ tsp salt and ¼ tsp pepper. Toss with cilantro and arugula; fold in steak. Serve with charred flour tortillas.

CHARRED SHRIMP, LEEK & ASPARAGUS SKEWERS

Stack skewers high with spring veggies and succulent shrimp
and serve with a slightly spicy sauce.

1	lb (21- to 25-count) peeled and deveined shrimp
1	lb asparagus, trimmed and cut into 2-in. pieces
2	medium leeks, white and light green parts only, cut into 3/4-in.-thick rounds
2	Tbsp olive oil
	Kosher salt and pepper
2	lemons, halved
1/2	cup mayonnaise
1 1/2	Tbsp harissa paste

Active time: 25 min.

Total time: 25 min.

Serves: 4

About 370 cal
28.5 g fat (4.5 g sat)
18 g pro
1,110 mg sodium
12 g carb
2 g fiber

1. Heat grill to medium-high. Thread shrimp, asparagus and leek rounds onto skewers. Brush lightly with oil and season with 1/2 tsp each salt and pepper.

2. Grill skewers until vegetables are tender and shrimp are opaque throughout, 3 to 4 min. per side.

3. Place lemons on grill alongside skewers, cut-sides down, and grill until charred, about 4 min.

4. Into small bowl, squeeze 2 tsp juice from 1 charred lemon half. Stir in mayonnaise and harissa to combine. Serve skewers with harissa mayo and remaining charred lemon halves.

GRILLED ITALIAN SAUSAGE & PEPPER PIE

You don't need a fancy brick oven to fire up the perfect sausage pizza.

Flour, for dusting

1   **lb pizza dough (thawed if frozen), left out at room temperature for 30 min.**

2   **tsp olive oil, divided**

2   **small bell peppers (1 red and 1 orange), quartered**

1   **Cubanelle pepper, quartered**

2   **sweet Italian sausage links (about 8 oz), halved lengthwise**

4   **oz part-skim mozzarella, shredded**

½   **small red onion, thinly sliced**

3   **pepperoncini peppers, thinly sliced**

Active time: 15 min.

Total time: 25 min.

Serves: 4

About 485 cal
19 g fat (6 g sat)
19 g pro
1,495 mg sodium
55 g carb
3 g fiber

1. Heat grill to medium-high. Lightly dust baking sheet with flour. On floured surface, shape dough into 14-in. round; place on prepared sheet. Brush dough with 1 tsp oil.

2. Place peppers and sausages, cut-sides down, on grill and cook, covered, 3 min. Turn and grill, covered, until sausages are cooked through and peppers are tender, 2 to 3 min. more. Transfer to cutting board; slice.

3. Transfer pizza dough to hot grill grate, oiled-side down, and cook, covered, until top begins to bubble and bottom is crisp, about 2 min. Brush top of dough with remaining 1 tsp oil.

4. Turn dough over and sprinkle grilled side with half of mozzarella, then all of onion. Top with peppers, sausage and pepperoncini; sprinkle with remaining cheese. Grill, covered, until bottom is golden brown and crisp and mozzarella has melted, about 3 min. Transfer to cutting board; cut into pieces to serve.

SWORDFISH WITH SUMMER SALAD

It's not summer without grilled seafood. This dish is so easy, you can enjoy the catch of the day every day, if you'd like.

3	large ears corn, husked
1	lb skinless swordfish or halibut, cut into 1-in. chunks
1	small zucchini, halved lengthwise
2	Tbsp olive oil, divided
2	tsp chili powder
	Kosher salt
2	15-oz cans chickpeas, rinsed
½	cup packed mint, chopped
3	Tbsp fresh lime juice

Active time: 25 min.

Total time: 25 min.

Serves: 4

About 500 cal
19 g fat (3 g sat)
34 g pro
735 mg sodium
55 g carb
12 g fiber

1. Heat grill to medium-high. Grill corn, turning occasionally, until charred in spots, 5 to 8 min.

2. Thread swordfish onto 8 skewers. Brush fish and zucchini with 1 Tbsp oil; sprinkle with chili powder and ½ tsp salt. Grill fish and zucchini, until fish is opaque throughout and zucchini is tender, 3 to 4 min. per side.

3. Cut corn off cobs, chop zucchini and toss with chickpeas, mint, lime juice, remaining Tbsp oil and ¼ tsp salt. Serve with kebabs.

SMOKY GRILLED CHICKEN WINGS

Nothing imparts a burst of flavor to your favorite wing recipe quite like a hot grill.
We used chipotle pepper in adobo to layer on extra smokiness.

1/2	cup ketchup
2	Tbsp cider vinegar
1	Tbsp dark brown sugar
2	tsp Worcestershire sauce
1	chipotle pepper in adobo, finely chopped
1/2	cup sour cream
1	lime
1/4	cup fresh cilantro, chopped
1	oz feta cheese, crumbled
3	lbs chicken wings (about 36) split
2	Tbsp olive oil, divided
	Kosher salt and pepper
4	ears corn, husked and halved

Active time: 20 min.

Total time: 30 min.

Serves: 4

About 460 cal
27 g fat (9 g sat)
1 g pro
20 mg sodium
41 g carb
2 g fiber

1. Heat grill to medium-low. In small bowl, combine ketchup, vinegar, sugar, Worcestershire sauce and chipotle.

2. Place sour cream in small bowl. Finely grate zest of lime on top, then squeeze in juice (about 2 Tbsp). Add cilantro and feta and mix to combine; set aside.

KITCHEN TIP *Swap the wings for 4 6-oz boneless, skinless chicken breasts to save 10 g of fat per serving. Grill until cooked through, 5 to 7 min. per side.*

3. In large bowl, toss wings with 1 Tbsp oil and ¼ tsp each salt and pepper. Brush remaining Tbsp oil on corn.

4. Grill chicken wings, covered, turning occasionally, 12 min.

5. Place corn on grill. Grill wings and corn, basting wings with some sauce and turning corn occasionally, until chicken is cooked through and corn is slightly charred, 4 to 6 min. Serve corn with wings, any remaining chipotle sauce and sour cream sauce, for dipping.

GRILLED CHICKEN CAPRESE

Adding chicken is a great way to turn a Caprese salad into a full-blown meal.

1	**Tbsp red wine vinegar**
3	**Tbsp plus 2 tsp olive oil**
	Kosher salt
	Black pepper
1	**small shallot, finely chopped**
1	**cup corn kernels (from 1 large ear, or frozen, thawed)**
1	**pint assorted colored grape or cherry tomatoes, halved**
4	**6-oz boneless, skinless chicken breasts**
2	**lbs assorted colored medium and large tomatoes, sliced**
6	**oz fresh mozzarella, sliced**
¼	**cup small fresh basil leaves**

Active time: 20 min.

Total time: 20 min.

Serves: 4

About 390 cal
12 g fat (2 g sat)
45 g pro
580 mg sodium
18 g carb
4 g fiber

1. Heat grill to medium-high. In medium bowl, whisk together vinegar, 3 Tbsp oil and ½ tsp each salt and pepper; stir in shallot. Add corn and grape tomatoes and toss to combine; set aside.

2. Rub chicken with remaining 2 tsp oil, season with ½ tsp salt and ¼ tsp pepper, and grill until just cooked through, 4 to 6 min. per side.

3. Arrange chicken, sliced tomatoes and mozzarella on platter. Spoon corn mixture and any juices from bowl over top, then sprinkle with basil.

SPICED GRILLED EGGPLANT WITH FRESH TOMATO SALAD

Full of fiber, potassium and antioxidants, this low-calorie recipe is perfect for your next barbecue. It's also a great keto option!

2	medium eggplants (about 1 lb each), sliced lengthwise ½ in. thick
4	Tbsp olive oil, divided
1	tsp ground coriander
1	tsp cayenne
	Kosher salt
2	Tbsp fresh lemon juice
2	Tbsp red wine vinegar
1½	cups assorted colored cherry or grape tomatoes, halved
2	small Fresno chiles or other hot chiles, finely chopped
¼	cup packed fresh mint leaves, finely chopped, plus more for serving
¼	cup low-fat Greek yogurt
2	Tbsp low-fat milk

Active time: 30 min.

Total time: 30 min.

Serves: 4

About 140 cal
10 g fat (1.5 g sat)
3 g pro
310 mg sodium
12 g carb
5 g fiber

1. Heat grill to medium. Brush eggplant with 3 Tbsp oil, then season with coriander, cayenne and ¼ tsp salt. Grill until tender, 5 to 6 min. per side.

2. Meanwhile, in medium bowl, whisk together lemon juice, vinegar, remaining Tbsp oil and ½ tsp salt; fold in tomatoes, chiles and mint.

3. Arrange eggplant on a large platter; top with tomato salad. Whisk together yogurt and milk and drizzle over vegetables. Sprinkle with mint leaves, if desired.

SWEET-AND-SPICY GRILLED STEAK LETTUCE CUPS

This protein-packed steak and crunchy romaine combo isn't just healthy,
it's a satisfying meal that's easy to whip up.

1/4	cup red pepper jelly
1	Tbsp rice vinegar
2	tsp low-sodium tamari or soy sauce
1	lb sirloin steak, trimmed and cut in half lengthwise
2	jalapeños
1	small head romaine lettuce or romaine heart, leaves separated
6	radishes, thinly sliced
1	large carrot, thinly sliced
1	cup fresh cilantro
4	scallions, thinly sliced

Active time: 20 min.

Total time: 20 min.

Serves: 4

About 235 cal
8 g fat (3 g sat)
26 g pro
195 mg sodium
14 g carb
2 g fiber

1. Heat grill to medium-high. Make glaze: In a small bowl, combine pepper jelly, vinegar and tamari.

2. Grill steak to desired doneness, 5 to 6 min. per side for medium-rare, basting with glaze during last 2 min. of cooking. Transfer to cutting board and brush with remaining glaze; let rest at least 5 min. before slicing.

3. While steak is grilling, grill jalapeños, turning occasionally, until lightly charred, about 3 min. Cut into 1/2-in. pieces.

4. Fill lettuce leaves with steak and top with jalapeños, radishes, carrot, cilantro and scallions.

CUMIN GRILLED SHRIMP & ASPARAGUS

This is the perfect summer night meal.

2	small navel oranges, 1 halved and 1 sliced into rounds
1	cup couscous
2	scallions, thinly sliced
	Kosher salt and pepper
1	lb thin asparagus, trimmed
1	Tbsp olive oil
1¼	lbs large (16 to 20 count) peeled and deveined shrimp
½	tsp ground cumin
¼	tsp cayenne

Active time: 25 min.

Total time: 25 min.

Serves: 4

About 335 cal
5 g fat (1 g sat)
31 g pro
505 mg sodium
45 g carb
5 g fiber

1. Heat grill to medium-high. Squeeze juice from one orange half into bowl (about ¼ cup). Add couscous, scallions and ¼ tsp salt, then 1 cup water, and let sit, covered, 15 min.

2. Meanwhile, toss asparagus with oil and ¼ tsp each salt and pepper. Season shrimp with cumin, cayenne and ¼ tsp salt.

3. Place asparagus, orange slices and remaining orange half on grill and cook until oranges are charred and asparagus is just tender, 2 to 3 min. per side; transfer to plate.

4. Add shrimp to grill and cook until opaque throughout, about 2 min. per side. Squeeze grilled orange half over shrimp just before they are done. Fluff couscous and serve with shrimp, asparagus and orange slices.

KITCHEN TIP *For even more flavor, rub the steak with the spices and refrigerate overnight.*

GRILLED MOROCCAN STEAK & CARROTS

The grill brings the smoke, but the cumin, coriander and cinnamon-rubbed steak bring the fire-boosted flavor.

1	cup packed cilantro
1	cup packed flat-leaf parsley, plus more for serving
1	tsp smoked paprika
1	large clove garlic
½	cup plus 1 Tbsp olive oil
1	tsp lemon zest plus 2 Tbsp lemon juice (from 1 lemon)
	Kosher salt and pepper
1	tsp ground cumin
1	tsp ground coriander
½	tsp ground cinnamon
1½	lbs sirloin steak, cut into 4 pieces
1	lb small carrots, scrubbed, halved lengthwise if thick
1	oz feta cheese, crumbled

Active time: 15 min.

Total time: 25 min.

Serves: 4

About 635 cal
46 g fat (11 g sat)
41 g pro
670 mg sodium
14 g carb
5 g fiber

1. Heat grill to medium. In blender, puree cilantro, parsley, paprika, garlic, ½ cup oil, lemon zest and juice, and ¼ tsp each salt and pepper. Transfer to small bowl.

2. Combine cumin, coriander and cinnamon with ¼ tsp salt and ½ tsp pepper; rub all over steak. Rub carrots with remaining Tbsp oil and season with ¼ tsp each salt and pepper.

3. Grill steak and carrots, covered, until carrots are tender and steak is medium-rare, 3 to 5 min. per side. Transfer steak to cutting board and let rest 5 min. before slicing.

4. Drizzle carrots with ¼ cup sauce and sprinkle with feta and parsley. Serve with steak and remaining sauce.

PORK WITH GRILLED SWEET POTATO "FRIES"

Paired with a spicy, bright salsa verde, this sweet and smoky dinner hits every craving.

1/3	cup walnuts
1	small clove garlic
1	small jalapeño, cut into pieces
1/2	cup mint leaves
1	Tbsp capers
	Kosher salt and pepper
1	Tbsp honey
1	Tbsp lemon juice
1/3	cup plus 2 Tbsp olive oil
3	large sweet potatoes, cut into 1-in. wedges
4	small pork chops (about 1 in. thick)

Active time: 20 min.

Total time: 30 min.

Serves: 4

About 540 cal
28.5 g fat (7 g sat)
44 g pro
440 mg sodium
26 g carb
5 g fiber

1. Heat grill to medium. In food processor, finely chop walnuts, garlic, jalapeño, mint, capers and pinch salt. Pulse in honey, lemon juice and 1/3 cup oil.

2. Toss sweet potatoes with 1 Tbsp olive oil and 1/4 tsp each salt and pepper. Brush pork chops with remaining Tbsp oil and season with 1/4 tsp each salt and pepper.

3. Grill pork and carrots, covered, until pork is just cooked through and potatoes are tender, 5 to 7 min. per side. Serve with salsa verde.

GRILLED CHICKEN & PLUM SALAD

Add peak-season plums alongside the chicken on the grill
for a hearty, fresh salad that's perfect for summer.

4	**6-oz boneless, skinless chicken breasts**
2	**Tbsp plus 1 tsp olive oil, divided**
	Kosher salt and pepper
4	**red plums, cut into 1-in. wedges**
2	**scallions, thinly sliced**
6	**cups baby arugula**
½	**cup fresh dill, very roughly chopped**
¼	**cup roasted almonds, chopped**

Active time: 20 min.

Total time: 20 min.

Serves: 4

About 355 cal
16.5 fat (2.5 g sat)
38 g pro
345 mg sodium
12 g carb
3 g fiber

1. Heat grill to medium. Rub chicken with 1 tsp olive oil and season with ¼ tsp each salt and pepper. In large bowl, toss plums with 1 Tbsp oil and ¼ tsp each salt and pepper.

2. Grill chicken until cooked through, 5 to 7 min. per side. Transfer to cutting board and let rest 5 min. before slicing.

3. Add plums to grill and cook until just charred, 2 to 3 min. per side; return to bowl and toss with remaining Tbsp oil and scallions.

4. Add chicken (and any juices) to bowl and toss to combine. Fold in arugula, dill and almonds.

PORK CHOPS WITH BLOODY MARY TOMATO SALAD

Fresh veggies seasoned with Worcestershire sauce, horseradish, Tabasco and celery seeds show that the flavors of a classic Bloody Mary can go beyond brunch.

2	**Tbsp olive oil**
2	**Tbsp red wine vinegar**
2	**tsp Worcestershire sauce**
2	**tsp prepared horseradish, squeezed dry**
1/2	**tsp hot sauce (we use Tabasco)**
1/2	**tsp celery seeds**
	Kosher salt and pepper
1	**pint cherry tomatoes, halved**
2	**stalks celery, very thinly sliced**
1/2	**small red onion, thinly sliced**
4	**small pork chops (1 in. thick, about 2¼ lbs total)**
1/4	**cup flat-leaf parsley, finely chopped**
1	**small head green-leaf lettuce, leaves torn**

Active time: 20 min.

Total time: 25 min.

Serves: 4

About 400 cal
23 g fat (6 g sat)
39 g pro
525 mg sodium
8 g carb
3 g fiber

1. Heat grill to medium-high. In large bowl, whisk together oil, vinegar, Worcestershire sauce, horseradish, hot sauce, celery seeds and ¼ tsp salt. Toss with tomatoes, celery and onion.

2. Season pork chops with ½ tsp each salt and pepper and grill until golden brown and just cooked through, 5 to 7 min. per side.

3. Fold parsley into tomatoes and serve over pork and greens.

STEAK & GRILLED PEPPERS WITH CHIMICHURRI

Bring this classic Argentinian sauce into your backyard BBQ for a flavor-packed steak topper that's great on grilled veggies, too.

1	lb assorted colored mini sweet peppers
3	Tbsp olive oil, divided
	Kosher salt and pepper
2	12-oz strip steaks (about 1½ in. thick), trimmed
2	Tbsp red wine vinegar
2	scallions, finely chopped
1	small clove garlic, grated
½	large red chile, seeded and finely chopped
½	cup flat-leaf parsley, chopped
½	cup fresh cilantro, chopped

Active time: 25 min.

Total time: 25 min.

Serves: 6

About 275 cal
16.5 g fat (4.5 g sat)
25 g pro
235 mg sodium
6 g carb
2 g fiber

1. Heat grill to medium. In large bowl, toss peppers with 1 Tbsp oil and ¼ tsp each salt and pepper. Season steaks with ¼ tsp each salt and pepper.

2. Grill steak and peppers, covered, turning peppers occasionally until peppers are lightly charred and tender, 5 to 7 min., and steak is cooked to desired doneness, 5 to 8 min. per side. Transfer peppers to platter and steak to cutting board and let rest at least 5 min. before slicing.

3. Meanwhile, in small bowl, combine vinegar, scallions, garlic, chile, remaining 2 Tbsp oil and pinch each salt and pepper. Stir in parsley and cilantro and serve with steak and peppers.

HONEY-GINGER CEDAR PLANK SALMON

The cedar plank both imparts incredible flavor and acts as a stunning serving board for the spicy-sweet salmon.

2   tsp lemon zest plus ¼ cup juice, plus slices, for serving
2   tsp grated peeled fresh ginger
      Kosher salt and pepper
1   large piece skin-on wild Alaskan salmon (about 2 lbs)
3   Tbsp low-sodium soy sauce
2   Tbsp honey
1   Tbsp sriracha
1   clove garlic, crushed with press
4   cups packed arugula, plus more for serving
4   Persian cucumbers, thinly sliced
1¼   cups corn kernels (from 2 ears or frozen, thawed)
½   cup cilantro leaves

Active time: 15 min.

Total time: 30 min.

Serves: 8

About 190 cal
5 g fat (1 g sat)
25 g pro
530 mg sodium
12 g carb
1 g fiber

1. Soak large cedar grilling plank (about 15- by 7-in.) in water 1 to 2 hr. Heat grill on medium.

2. Combine zest, ginger, ½ tsp each salt and pepper and rub all over flesh side of salmon. Place salmon, skin-side down on soaked plank and grill, covered until opaque throughout, 20 to 25 min.

3. Meanwhile, in medium bowl, whisk soy sauce, honey and sriracha; set aside half. To remaining soy mixture, add garlic, reserved lemon juice and ¼ tsp salt; toss with arugula, cucumbers, corn and cilantro. Brush salmon with reserved soy mixture. Top with arugula and lemon slices, if desired. Serve with cucumber salad.

GRILLED CHICKEN WITH SMOKY CORN SALAD

Not your average corn salad: Charred lime, cilantro, green olives and Manchego cheese bring something new to the (picnic) table.

4	**6-oz boneless, skinless chicken breast halves**
	Kosher salt and pepper
2	**limes, halved**
4	**ears corn, shucked**
¼	**cup cilantro, chopped**
2	**Tbsp chopped green olives**
1	**oz Manchego cheese, finely grated**
1½	**Tbsp olive oil**
1	**tsp smoked paprika**

Active time: 10 min.

Total time: 30 min.

Serves: 4

About 355 cal
13 g fat (3.5 g sat)
21 g pro
315 mg sodium
21 g carb
2 g fiber

1. Heat grill to medium-high. Season chicken with ¼ tsp each salt and pepper and grill until cooked through, 5 to 6 min. per side.

2. Meanwhile, grill limes, cut-sides down, and corn, turning occasionally, until charred, 1 min. for limes and 6 to 8 min. for corn.

3. Cut corn from cob and transfer to a bowl. Squeeze in juice of 2 lime halves, add cilantro, olives, Manchego cheese, and pinch each salt and pepper and toss to combine.

4. In small bowl, combine oil and paprika. Serve chicken with corn and remaining lime halves and drizzle with paprika oil.

APRICOT GRILLED PORK TENDERLOIN & PEPPERS

We're fired up about the apricot jam and white wine vinegar glaze
that locks in flavor to this juicy grilled pork.

4	bell peppers (red, yellow or a combination), quartered
1	red onion, cut into 1/2-in. wedges
1	Tbsp oil
	Kosher salt and pepper
2	small pork tenderloins, about 3/4 lb each
1/4	cup apricot jam
2	Tbsp white wine vinegar

Active time: 10 min.

Total time: 25 min.

Serves: 4

About 320 cal
9 g fat (2.5 g sat)
36 g pro
335 mg sodium
23 g carb
3 g fiber

1. Heat grill to medium-high. Toss bell peppers and onion
with oil and season with 1/4 tsp each salt and pepper.

2. Season pork tenderloins with 1/4 tsp each salt and pepper.
Grill vegetables and pork, covered, turning occasionally, until
vegetables are tender, 8 to 10 min. Transfer vegetables to
cutting board.

3. In small bowl, mix together jam and vinegar. Continue
grilling pork, basting with sauce until cooked through (145°F),
3 to 6 min. Let rest 5 min. before slicing. Coarsely chop
peppers and serve with onion, pork and any remaining sauce.

Corn on the Cob, recipe on p 199

5

BONUS:
AWESOME AIR FRYER

An air fryer is similar to an oven in the sense that it bakes and roasts, but the difference is its heating elements are only located on top and are accompanied by a large, powerful fan, resulting in food that's super crispy in no time. The best part? You get the same crunch using less oil than deep-fried counterparts.

If you haven't jumped on the air fryer train yet, here's the perfect excuse to do so. It is worth the counter real estate. Not only is it the healthier option to satisfy that deep-fried crunch craving, it's also a great way to get more done in the kitchen in less time. Use it to whip up a side of veggies while your main dish roasts in the oven or get a head start on dessert (our Individual Apple Pies, p. 204, take just 25 min. to cook up).

AIR FRYER MUST-HAVES

● **THE RIGHT STYLE.** Basket air fryers are optimal for heating large batches of food that can easily be shaken during cooking, but offer limited surface area when cooking in one layer. Air fryer ovens offer a solution to single-layer cooking with multiple shelves, but sometimes can be considered limiting for foods that need to be tossed often. They often feature additional accessories like a rotating basket and rotisserie spit. Toaster oven air fryers can air fry and perform all the functions of a typical toaster oven.

- ⚙ **A CONVENIENT SIZE.** Air fryers range in size from under two quarts to larger than seven quarts. Shop for the size that best suits the amount of portions you normally cook and the amount of cabinet storage you have.
- ⚙ **OIL DISPENSERS.** Little to no oil is needed to crisp up foods in the air fryer. When necessary, use a refillable spray bottle or a silicone basting brush to evenly coat foods with a small amount. Avoid propellant-based sprays that are often loaded with fillers that affect taste and non-stickability of trays.
- ⚙ **COOKING TOOLS.** Many air fryer baskets contain a nonstick coating that can easily be scratched and damaged by metal utensils. Choose heat resistant plastic or silicone options instead.

SECRETS TO (CRUNCHY) SUCCESS

For the best results every time, use these tips and tricks.

BEFORE AIR-FRYING

CUT FOOD INTO CONSISTENTLY SIZED PIECES to promote even cooking.

BRUSH THE TRAY WITH OIL OR USE A REFILLABLE SPRAY BOTTLE rather than using nonstick cooking spray. Propellants in nonstick spray can leave residue, which sticks to food during cooking.

DON'T OVERCROWD THE FRYER BASKET, and arrange foods in a single layer when possible to ensure a light, crispy exterior rather than a soggy one.

PACKAGED FROZEN FOODS don't need additional oil before being air-fried; they're usually already coated with numerous browning agents.

YOU CAN USE YOUR AIR FRYER to reheat foods. Place food in the basket and set the temperature to 300°F for 5 to 8 min. Remember to keep a close eye on it—foods reheat quickly.

WHILE AIR-FRYING

GENTLY SHAKE smaller ingredients in the fryer basket halfway through cooking (or every 5 to 10 min.) to help cook them evenly and enhance their crispy texture.

FLIP FOODS that are more than an inch thick halfway through cooking.

MOST AIR FRYER MODELS have a basket with a nonstick coating, so to preserve the finish, avoid scraping the surface with metal utensils.

IT'S OK TO PULL THE BASKET OUT at any time during the cooking cycle to check on the progress – most models will automatically shut off while the basket is out and resume when it's pushed back in. If food isn't sufficiently fried when the timer goes off, set the timer for a few extra min. and continue cooking.

AFTER AIR-FRYING

ALWAYS SET THE BASKET and any accessories on a heat-resistant surface when air-frying is complete. Use caution as these tools get very hot during the cooking process.

USE TONGS to lift large or delicate foods out of the fryer basket after air-frying. Otherwise, you can often turn food out directly onto a serving bowl or platter.

ONCE FOOD IS REMOVED, the air fryer is ready for another batch. But if you've been prepping fatty ingredients and excess oil has collected in the bottom, carefully pour it out.

CARE & CLEANING

Follow these easy instructions to keep your air fryer looking and smelling like new, but first be sure that the appliance is turned off, unplugged and cool.

CLEANING THE AIR FRYER BASKET AND RACK

1. Fill the basket with hot water and add a few drops of dishwashing soap. Let soak for 10 min.
2. Wash the basket walls and bottom, as well as the rack, with a moist cloth or a nonabrasive sponge.
3. Allow both the basket and rack to air-dry before putting them back into the device. Many models have dishwasher-safe parts.

WASHING THE EXTERIOR

Clean the outside of the air fryer, along with the walls of the interior cavity that holds the fryer basket, with a moist cloth. If necessary, when cool, remove food residue stuck to the heating element with a very damp nonabrasive sponge or a soft-bristled brush.

Avoid using steel wool or a hard-bristle brush, as these could damage the coating on the heating element.

AIR FRYER COOKING GUIDE

Reference the chart below for average cooking times of our favorite air fryer-friendly foods.

FOOD	TEMP	TIME	TIP
Baked Potato	400°F	25 min. or until tender	Pierce skin of potato before cooking
Bread/Rolls	350°F	15 to 25 min.	Air fry until browned and internal temp is about 200°F
Cake	330°F	15 to 25 min.	Ensure pan fits in air fryer before preparing
Chicken Breasts	380°F	10 to 15 min.	Brush lightly with oil before air frying; arrange in a single layer
Chicken Drumsticks	400°F	15 to 20 min.	Arrange in a single layer; flip toward the end of cooking
Chicken Nuggets	400°F	8 to 12 min.	Make sure they are arranged in a single layer
Fish	400°F	8 to 10 min.	Brush lean cuts and skin with oil
Frozen Fries	400°F	12 to 20 min.	Shake halfway through
Frozen Snacks (spring rolls, chicken wings, fish fillets, onion rings, etc.)	400°F	8 to 14 min. or until hot	Shake halfway through
Hamburger	400°F	8 to 12 min.	May need to flip depending on thickness
Homemade Fries	400°F	15 to 24 min.	Shake halfway through
Meatballs	400°F	10 to 12 min.	Shake occasionally
Mixed Veggies	400°F	8 to 12 min.	Shake halfway through
Muffins	350°F	8 to 12 min.	Use individual heat-proof baking cups to maximize cooking area; leave sufficient room between cups for muffins to expand during cooking
Pork Chops	400°F	8 to 14 min.	Flip halfway through
Potato Wedges	400°F	15 to 20 min.	Shake halfway through
Quiche	330°F	15 to 22 min.	Ensure pan fits in air fryer before preparing
Shrimp	400°F	10 to 12 min.	Shake occasionally and air fry until just until opaque throughout

AIR FRYER RECIPES

CRISPY FISH TACOS

We love mahi-mahi or tilapia in this recipe, but any mild white fish would work.
Save the bold flavor for crazy colorful toppings!

1/3	cup mayonnaise
2	Tbsp milk
1	tsp chili powder
1/4	tsp garlic powder
1 1/2	cups panko
4	tsp canola or vegetable oil, plus more oil for misting or brushing
	Kosher salt
1	lb skinless mahi-mahi or tilapia fillets, cut into 3-in.-long strips (1 in. wide)
	Small flour tortillas

Active time: 20 min.

Total time: 30 min.

Serves: 4

Fish only:
About 370 cal
19 g fat (3 g sat)
24 g pro
525 mg sodium
23 g carb
1 g fiber

1. In small bowl, whisk together mayonnaise, milk, chili powder and garlic powder. On plate, mix panko with oil and 1/2 tsp salt.

2. Working with a few strips at a time, toss fish in mayonnaise mixture to coat and then in panko, pressing to help adhere. Place coated strips on baking sheet.

3. Spray or brush basket with oil. In two batches, arrange fish with space between strips and stack strips perpendicularly in the second layer. Air fry at 390°F until cooked through, 4 to 5 min. per batch.

4. Serve on flour tortillas with your choice of toppings (at right).

FUN TOPPING FLAVORS

PINEAPPLE & ROMAINE SLAW

In bowl, toss **¼ small pineapple** (cut into ¼-in. pieces) and **2 scallions** (thinly sliced) with **1 Tbsp each lime juice** and **olive oil** and **¼ tsp each salt** and **pepper**. Toss with **½ heart romaine lettuce** (shredded; about 1½ cups) and **¼ cup cilantro** (chopped).

CITRUSY RADISHES

In bowl, whisk together **1 Tbsp each orange juice** and **lemon juice** and **¼ tsp each ground cumin**, **salt** and **pepper**. Toss with **6 radishes** (very thinly sliced) and **¼ small sweet onion** (thinly sliced). Fold in **¼ cup cilantro**.

CABBAGE SLAW

In bowl, whisk together **2 Tbsp each sour cream** and **lime juice**, **⅛ tsp cayenne** and **¼ tsp salt**. Toss with **2 cups shredded green or red cabbage**. Let stand, tossing often, 10 min. Stir in **1 scallion** (sliced) and **2 Tbsp cilantro** (chopped).

SAUSAGE CALZONES

Melty on the inside with a mouthwatering sausage, pea and ricotta filling and crispy on the outside, this is the tastiest way to transform store-bought sauce and pizza dough.

1	**cup part-skim ricotta cheese**
1	**link fully cooked Italian chicken sausage (3 oz), diced**
3/4	**cup frozen peas**
1/2	**cup shredded part-skim mozzarella cheese**
1	**lb refrigerated pizza dough, at room temp**
1	**cup marinara sauce, warmed**

Active time: 15 min.

Total time: 30 min.

Serves: 4

About 470 cal
14 g fat (5 g sat)
22 g pro
1,440 mg sodium
60 g carb
4 g fiber

1. In medium bowl, stir together ricotta, sausage, peas and mozzarella.

2. Divide dough into 4 pieces and shape each into 7-in.-wide oval.

3. Place ¼ of ricotta filling on half of each piece of dough. Brush rim of dough with water and fold other half over filling. Pinch edges together to seal.

4. In 2 batches, air fry at 360°F, turning over with tongs halfway through, until golden brown and heated through, 12 min. Serve with marinara sauce.

HOT DOGS WITH TOPPERS

Enjoy the crispiness of classic summer dogs without turning on the grill.

4 hot dogs
4 hot dog buns
  Toppings (recipe below)

Place hot dogs in air fryer basket. Air fry at 390°F until lightly browned and heated through, 6 min. Serve on buns and top as desired.

Active time: 10 min.

Total time: 15 min.

Serves: 4

About 285 cal
17 g fat (6 g sat)
10 g pro
635 mg sodium
23 g carb
1 g fiber

HOT DOG TOPPERS

CLASSIC DOG
2 Tbsp sweet stewed onions
1 Tbsp sauerkraut
1 Tbsp yellow mustard

ITALIAN DOG
1 oz sautéed peppers and onions
1 oz roasted potato chunks

SONORAN DOG
2 Tbsp fresh pico de gallo
1 Tbsp pickled or fresh jalapeños
1 Tbsp sour cream
Cilantro

CUBAN FRITA DOG
2 Tbsp potato sticks
1½ Tbsp chopped raw white onion
1 Tbsp ketchup

HAWAIIAN DOG
2 tsp yellow mustard
1 Tbsp garlic mayo
2 Tbsp finely chopped fresh pineapple
1 Tbsp sliced scallions

FISH 'N' CHIPS

Flaky cod gets dipped into—wait for it—salt and vinegar chips for the crispiest-ever coating that's a fun play on a classic dish.

1½   lbs cod fillet
3   large egg whites, beaten
6   oz salt-and-vinegar potato chips, finely crushed
        Olive oil, for misting or brushing
        Kosher salt and pepper
1   lb frozen peas
3   Tbsp unsalted butter
1   Tbsp lemon juice
        Lemon wedges and chives, for serving

Active time: 10 min.

Total time: 30 min.

Serves: 4

About 320 cal
25 g fat (8 g sat)
39 g pro
775 mg sodium
40 g carb
7 g fiber

1. Cut fish into equal-size pieces; fold thinner tail ends in half if needed and secure with toothpicks. Dip cod into egg whites, then chips, pressing to help adhere. Spray or brush with oil.

2. Working in 2 batches, place fish in basket and air fry at 350°F until golden brown and opaque throughout, 8 to 10 min. Sprinkle with salt.

3. Meanwhile, microwave frozen peas, butter, lemon juice and ¼ tsp each salt and pepper on High 5 min. Transfer to food processor and purée. Serve with fish and lemon wedges and chives, if desired.

KITCHEN TIP *Crush chips right in the bag for less mess. Make a small hole in the top (so air can escape) and go to town with a rolling pin.*

CHICKEN CAPRESE

The fresh tomato and mozzarella salad, plus a side of bright
Broccolini, lightens up this Italian classic.

1	**cup grape tomatoes, halved**
1	**clove garlic, pressed**
2	**tsp olive oil, divided**
	Kosher salt and pepper
2	**thin-cut boneless, skinless chicken breasts**
4	**oz fresh mozzarella balls, halved**
¼	**cup fresh basil, torn**
1	**bunch Broccolini, steamed, for serving**

Active time: 10 min.

Total time: 25 min.

Serves: 2

About 430 cal
24 g fat (10 g sat)
43 g pro
380 mg sodium
11 g carb
4 g fiber

1. In bowl, toss tomatoes with garlic, 1 tsp oil and pinch each
of salt and pepper. Place in basket and air fry at 400°F until
tomatoes are tender and some burst, 3 to 4 min. Remove from
basket and transfer to bowl; set aside.

2. Brush chicken with remaining tsp oil and sprinkle with ⅛ tsp
each salt and pepper. Air fry at 400°F until cooked through,
5 to 6 min. Transfer cutlets to plates.

3. Fold mozzarella and basil into tomatoes and spoon over
chicken. Serve with Broccolini, if desired.

ZUCCHINI TOTS

These spudless, cheesy-on-the-inside bites are about to become your favorite way to use up extra summer squash.

2	medium zucchini (about 12 oz)
1	large egg
½	cup grated Pecorino Romano cheese
½	cup panko
1	clove garlic, grated
	Pepper
	Olive oil, for misting or brushing

Active time: 15 min.

Total time: 30 min.

Serves: 4 (6 tots each)

About 140 cal
6 g fat (4 g sat)
10 g pro
300 mg sodium
10 g carb
2 g fiber

1. Using box grater, coarsely grate zucchini; squeeze out excess moisture. Transfer to large bowl. Mix with egg, Pecorino Romano, panko, garlic and ¼ tsp pepper.

2. With small cookie scoop, drop tablespoonfuls onto cutting board, and shape into 1-in. logs.

3. Spray or brush basket with oil. Place half of the tots in basket at a time and air fry each batch at 375°F, shaking occasionally, until golden brown, 6 min.

CHICKPEA "NUTS"

Sprinkle them over salads or add them to soups to take dinner to the next level.

2   15-oz cans chickpeas, rinsed
1   Tbsp olive oil
     Kosher salt and pepper

Active time: 10 min.

Total time: 25 min.

Serves: 8 (¼ cup each)

About 105 cal
3 g fat (0 g sat)
5 g pro
200 mg sodium
15 g carb
4 g fiber

1. Place chickpeas on paper towels to absorb any excess water. In bowl, toss chickpeas with oil and ¼ tsp each salt and pepper until evenly coated.

2. Place chickpeas in basket and air fry at 400°F, shaking basket twice, until crisp, 23 min. Remove from fryer and transfer to bowl; toss with seasonings (variations below) if desired. Chickpeas will continue to crisp as they cool. Cool completely and store in air-tight container.

FUN FLAVORS

HONEY-SESAME
Toss roasted chickpeas in **2 Tbsp honey**; **1 Tbsp each sesame oil, sesame seeds** and **sugar**; and **½ tsp each garlic powder** and **five-spice powder**. Using foil, line bottom and ½ in. up side of air fryer basket. Spray or brush with **olive oil** and add coated chickpeas. Air fry at 400°F until caramelized and crisp, 6 to 8 min., shaking basket twice.

BBQ
Toss roasted chickpeas in **1 tsp dark brown sugar** and **½ tsp each ground cumin, smoked paprika, garlic powder** and **chili powder**.

MASALA
Toss roasted chickpeas in **½ tsp each garam masala, ground cumin** and **ground ginger** and **¼ tsp cayenne**. Return to air fryer 4 min. until dry and crisp.

MAPLE-CINNAMON
Toss roasted chickpeas in **2 Tbsp maple syrup, 2 tsp sugar, 1 tsp ground cinnamon** and **¼ tsp ground nutmeg**. Return to air fryer 5 min. until caramelized and crisp.

PARMESAN-HERB
Toss roasted chickpeas in **¼ cup finely grated Parmesan** and **1 tsp each garlic powder, finely chopped fresh rosemary** and **loosely packed lemon zest**.

SPICE-ROASTED CARROTS

Say goodbye to sad steamed veggies once and for all. For a pop of color,
look for rainbow carrots, sometimes called heirloom carrots.

6	carrots (about 1¼ lbs), halved crosswise and lengthwise
1	Tbsp olive oil
1	Tbsp packed fresh oregano leaves, chopped
½	tsp smoked paprika
¼	tsp ground nutmeg
	Kosher salt and pepper
1	Tbsp unsalted butter, melted
½	Tbsp red wine vinegar
2	Tbsp roasted, salted shelled pistachios, chopped

Active time: 15 min.

Total time: 30 min.

Serves: 4

About 135 cal
8 g fat (6 g sat)
3 g pro
270 mg sodium
14 g carb
4 g fiber

1. In large bowl, toss together carrots, oil, oregano, paprika, nutmeg, ¼ tsp salt and ⅛ tsp pepper.

2. Place carrots in air fryer basket. Air fry at 370°F, shaking basket twice, until lightly browned and tender, 15 min.

3. Transfer to serving platter. Drizzle with butter and vinegar and sprinkle with pistachios.

KITCHEN TIP *Don't use large carrots for this recipe; they're tough to fit in the air fryer!*

CRISPY KALE "CHIPS"

An air fryer makes it easy to get a golden-brown crisp
on these chili-garlic "chips."

8	**cups deribbed kale leaves, torn into 2-in. pieces**
1½	**Tbsp olive oil**
¾	**tsp chili powder**
½	**tsp paprika**
¼	**tsp garlic powder**
2	**tsp sesame seeds**

Active time: 15 min.

Total time: 25 min.

Serves: 5 (1 cup each)

About 60 cal
5 g fat (1 g sat)
1 g pro
25 mg sodium
3 g carb
1 g fiber

1. In large bowl, toss together kale, oil, chili powder, paprika, garlic powder and sesame seeds. Massage kale 1 min.

2. Place in basket and air fry at 350°F, turning twice with tongs, until crisp, 8 min.

3. Let cool and store in air-tight container up to 1 week.

KITCHEN TIP *Don't tear the kale too small — as it dehydrates, smaller pieces can easily be blown around inside the air fryer.*

CHIMICHURRI CAULIFLOWER "STEAKS"

We treat the versatile veggie just like our favorite proteins, with a golden-brown crust and a punchy herb sauce for serving on top.

1	**large head cauliflower (about 2 lbs)**
1	**tsp ground cumin**
3	**Tbsp canola oil, divided**
	Kosher salt
¼	**cup loosely packed cilantro, finely chopped**
¼	**cup loosely packed parsley, finely chopped**
3	**Tbsp red wine vinegar**
1	**small clove garlic, crushed with press**
1	**jalapeño, seeded and finely chopped**

Active time: 10 min.

Total time: 20 min.

Serves: 4

About 120 cal
11 g fat (1 g sat)
2 g pro
210 mg sodium
5 g carb
2 g fiber

1. Quarter cauliflower and slice into ¾-in. slabs. Combine cumin, 1 Tbsp oil and ¼ tsp salt in large bowl. Toss in cauliflower until evenly coated.

2. Place cauliflower in basket and air fry at 390°F, shaking basket twice during cooking, until tender and browned, 16 min.

3. Meanwhile, combine cilantro, parsley, vinegar, garlic, jalapeño, remaining 2 Tbsp oil and ⅛ tsp salt. Spoon over cauliflower.

FUN FLAVORS

Skip the butter and spread one of these condiments on your corn instead—harissa, garlic-herb cheese spread, pimiento cheese or pesto.

CORN ON THE COB

Savor sweet, juicy corn without having to turn on the grill or the stove.

4 **ears corn, shucked**
Paprika, sour cream and chives, for serving

Trim corn, if needed, to fit air fryer and place in basket. Air fry at 375°F, turning over with tongs halfway through, until tender, 12 min. Serve with paprika, sour cream and chives, if desired.

Active time: 5 min.

Total time: 20 min.

Serves: 4

About 90 cal
1 g fat (0 g sat)
3 g pro
15 mg sodium
19 g carb
2 g fiber

KITCHEN TIP *Whether you're cooking one or four ears of corn, the timing for this recipe is the same.*

BAKED RICOTTA

Stash the leftovers in the fridge to use as a sandwich spread for the rest of the week.

1	15-oz container whole-milk ricotta cheese
3	Tbsp grated Parmesan cheese, divided
2	Tbsp extra virgin olive oil
1	tsp fresh thyme leaves, chopped
1	tsp grated lemon zest
1	clove garlic, crushed with press
	Kosher salt and pepper
	Toasted Baguette Slices (recipe below) or crackers, for serving

Active time: 10 min.

Total time: 25 min.

Makes: 2 cups

Each cup about 135 cal
11 g fat (5 g sat)
7 g pro
139 mg sodium
2 g carb
0 g fiber

1. In large bowl, whisk together ricotta, 2 Tbsp Parmesan, oil, thyme, lemon zest, garlic and ¼ tsp each salt and pepper. Transfer to a 6-in. 3-cup ovenproof baking dish; cover dish tightly with foil.

2. Air fry at 380°F for 10 min. Remove foil cover and sprinkle with remaining Tbsp Parmesan. Air fry until top is brown and bubbly at edges, 5 min. more. Use mitts to carefully remove from air fryer. Serve warm with Toasted Baguette Slices or crackers.

KITCHEN TIP *To make toasted baguette slices, toast twelve ¼-in.-thick baguette slices at a time. Spray or brush 1 side of each slice with olive oil. Air fry at 350°F 4 to 5 min., tossing a few times with tongs, until lightly toasted. Repeat in batches if needed.*

SHORTCUT JELLY DONUTS

Hot, fresh donuts? Now, that's our jam. Make them at home in minutes with our fried-and-true recipe.

1	16.3-oz pkg. large refrigerated biscuits
	Olive oil, for misting or brushing
1¼	cups raspberry jam
	Confectioners' sugar, for dusting

Active time: 10 min.

Total time: 25 min.

Serves: 8

About 305 cal
6 g fat (3 g sat)
3 g pro
460 mg sodium
59 g carb
1 g fiber

1. Separate biscuits into 8 rounds. Lightly spray or brush both sides with oil.

2. Spray or brush basket with oil and place 3 to 4 biscuits in basket. Air fry at 350°F until golden brown, 5 min. Transfer to wire rack; let cool. Repeat with remaining biscuits.

3. Fit a pastry bag with a small round tip, and fill with raspberry jam; use tip to poke a small hole in the center of each donut, then fill with jam. Dust donuts with confectioners' sugar.

INDIVIDUAL APPLE PIES

Ditch the pie pan! Line ramekins with crust and make mini personalized pies, because no one will want to share.

Flour, for surface
1	refrigerated rolled pie crust
1	lb McIntosh apples
2	Tbsp packed brown sugar
2	Tbsp dried cranberries
2	tsp all-purpose flour
1/2	tsp ground cinnamon
1/8	tsp grated nutmeg
1/4	tsp grated orange zest
	Kosher salt

Active time: 15 min.

Total time: 25 min. plus cooling

Serves: 3

About 345 cal
14 g fat (6 g sat)
3 g pro
335 mg sodium
58 g carb
2 g fiber

1. On lightly floured surface, roll pie crust to 14 in. in diameter. Cut out three 4½-in. rounds and place on baking sheet; refrigerate.

2. Peel, halve, core and thinly slice apples. In microwave-safe bowl, toss apples, brown sugar, cranberries, flour, cinnamon, nutmeg, orange zest and pinch salt. Microwave on High 2½ min. or just until softened, stirring once.

3. Divide filling among three 6-oz (3½-in.-diameter) ramekins. Place pie crust rounds on top and cut slits in centers. Place in air fryer basket and air fry at 350°F until golden brown, 10 to 12 min. Let cool 10 min. before serving.

KITCHEN TIP *Make a double batch and store at room temp for a day or refrigerate up to 2 days. Microwave apples on High 6 min., stirring twice. Then air fry in 2 batches.*

THANK YOU

For Purchasing Good Housekeeping's Easy 30-Minute Dinners.

If you'd like to expand your Good Housekeeping library with cookbooks, meal plans and more, visit our store at **Shop.GoodHousekeeping.com**

PHOTO CREDITS